OECD Public Governance Reviews

National Schools of Government

BUILDING CIVIL SERVICE CAPACITY

Please cite this publication as:
OECD (2017), *National Schools of Government: Building Civil Service Capacity*, OECD Public Governance Reviews, OECD Publishing, Paris.
http://dx.doi.org/10.1787/9789264268906-en

ISBN 978-92-64-26889-0 (print)
ISBN 978-92-64-26890-6 (PDF)

Series: OECD Public Governance Reviews
ISSN 2219-0406 (print)
ISSN 2219-0414 (online)

Photo credits: Cover © Ellagrin/ Shutterstock.com

Corrigenda to OECD publications may be found on line at: *www.oecd.org/about/publishing/corrigenda.htm*.

Foreword

Governments around the world are under increased pressure to become more transparent, open and accountable, and build institutions that are responsive to citizens' aspirations to restore or maintain trust in government. Effective implementation of these priorities strongly depends on the competencies and capabilities of public servants in national administrations.

Schools of government are uniquely placed to enhance the capacity of public servants to meet the leadership, policy and delivery challenges they face. Schools play this role both directly, through their learning and training programmes, and indirectly, by encouraging a learning culture that contributes to civil service effectiveness and efficiency. However, to remain relevant and responsive, schools also need to adapt their programmes to the changing needs of governments and civil servants.

What are the main achievements and challenges of national schools of government in promoting civil service learning and developing the right skills for meeting citizens' expectations? How do schools of government ensure responsiveness to government priorities in learning programmes? What are the schools' capacities, management models and innovative methods to enable public service learning?

This publication reviews how members of the OECD Global Network of Schools of Government are addressing these questions and presents a comprehensive analysis of best practices and common challenges. Established in 2014, the OECD Global Network of Schools of Government provides direct access to OECD governance expertise, and allows schools to exchange experiences and good practices in ensuring that public sector employees have the skills and competencies to address current and future priorities.

The report is part of the Network's efforts to create a dialogue across OECD and partner countries on effective and innovative tools in shaping public service delivery including capacity building, policy implementation and research needs. It draws on the results of the 2014 OECD Survey of National Schools of Government, the first cross-national OECD study of these institutions, and contributes to international comparative knowledge in this area. The report highlights that, while classroom teaching remains the preferred training method, there is a growing trend toward new training modalities, such as online training, team-based activities and study tours. These innovations are mainly driven by changes in civil service demographics – new civil service recruits often have different learning needs – as well as by fiscal pressures and the need to demonstrate results and value for money. The report finds that further investments in monitoring and evaluation activities are essential for ensuring enhanced impact and relevance of schools of government programmes.

The report includes recommendations on designing and implementing whole-of-government and organisation-specific civil service learning and development strategies. It also makes recommendations for improving schools' effectiveness through a greater focus on training programmes and evaluation processes. The report suggests steps to ensure the alignment of learning programmes with the priorities of national governments, enhance innovative techniques in the delivery and content of learning and development, as well as to foster their stable and adequate funding.

Acknowledgements

The report was prepared by the Governance Reviews and Partnerships Division, led by Martin Forst, of the Public Governance and Territorial Development Directorate, headed by Rolf Alter. The report was elaborated under the strategic direction of Tatyana Teplova, Senior Analyst and Deputy Head of Governance Reviews and Partnerships Division. The report was drafted by Michael O'Neill, Policy Analyst, and Evgenia Korotkova, Policy Analyst. Edwin Lau, Head of the Reform of the Public Sector Division, and Daniel Gerson, Project Manager, provided significant contributions to the report and to the 2014 OECD Survey of National Schools of Government. Editorial work and quality control were done by Julie Harris and Andrea Uhrhammer. Ciara Muller prepared the manuscript for publication. Administrative support was provided by Makeda Yohannes, Isabelle Reullon and Katarzyna Weil.

The OECD Secretariat wishes to thank members of the Steering Committee of the OECD Global Network of Schools of Government for their valuable guidance and support, particularly their Chair, Professor Tria, Director of the National School of Administration of Italy. The OECD wishes to acknowledge the significant contribution made by all members of the network and respondents to the 2014 OECD Survey. The team is grateful for the insightful comments and support provided by delegates of the OECD Public Governance Committee.

Table of contents

Tables

Figures

Figures *(continued)*

Boxes

Boxes *(continued)*

Executive summary

In the wake of global crisis, public administrations around the world struggle to find equilibrium between fiscal austerity and citizens' expectations about how to address current and emerging challenges, such as the migration crisis, climate change and ageing populations. Governments also need to adapt their political and managerial agendas to the pace of technology and innovation, growing budgetary pressures, and civil society's increasing demand for public and media scrutiny of decision making, spending and performance. Achieving such change – and stimulating inclusive economic growth and social well-being – requires an efficient and resilient civil service able to make strategic choices and be armed with fit-for-purpose skills.

Encouraging learning and skills development becomes a strategic choice for governments

Schools of government are uniquely positioned to play a central role in developing the necessary skills and competencies to meet government needs and priorities. However, further efforts are needed to align their learning and development programmes with government priorities. The schools need more robust, comprehensive and regular channels of dialogue with government, as well as with a broader set of non-governmental stakeholders, to ensure that civil servants have the knowledge and know-how skills to deal with current and emerging policy issues.

Innovation and quality assurance in learning programmes are essential to ensure their responsiveness

Fiscal pressures, citizens' rising expectations and strong competition from other training providers are compelling schools to explore innovative programmes and learning methods, such as e-learning. There is a growing emphasis on ensuring programme quality, including through regular learning and training programme reviews and accreditations. These strategies can help ensure responsiveness to the needs of individual learners and the government as a whole, while achieving cost savings and efficiencies. Yet, progress appears relatively slow, though the pace, types and approaches to adopting innovative training and development techniques vary significantly across schools. The impact of these innovations on learning outcomes and on the increased ability of schools to respond to government priorities is still to be assessed.

Monitoring and evaluation is an essential but underutilised tool

Evaluation results – both positive and negative – can contribute to review and renewal. In an environment in which government institutions must increasingly demonstrate their effectiveness and efficiency, schools are under pressure to demonstrate return on investment in education. This can be a challenge, given the diffused way that potential benefits may manifest. Many schools have several mechanisms for assessing the quality of their programmes; these are mainly internally managed, such as through participant surveys. Schools can thus strengthen the monitoring and evaluation of all their activities, including research, in order to demonstrate how these contribute to institutional and government goals and priorities. Doing so may require schools to move toward independent evaluations that are based on an extended range of tools and inputs and that focus on both outputs and longer-term outcomes, such as ex post evaluations of employee performance management.

Effective schools' governance and management are critical to ensure relevance of their programmes to government priorities and civil service capacity needs

Differing national contexts and policy preferences regarding governance, management and administration explain the different governance models among schools of government. Yet, it is important to ensure that the schools' governance model allows for the proper and efficient administration of the institution; provides clarity as to the school's mandate, roles and responsibilities; and ensures responsiveness to the needs of clients and the government as a whole. Establishing clear and robust co-ordination mechanisms with governmental and non-governmental stakeholders will also be essential to ensure that learning and development programmes strengthen the capacity of the civil service, especially for schools with higher degrees of autonomy.

Similar to other public institutions, schools are under pressure to achieve more with less and demonstrate value for money

Looking to the future, schools of government will need to find ways to provide value for money by demonstrating greater agility in adapting their curricula to changing civil service needs and developing innovative approaches to learning and development. Since all aspects of the schools are interrelated – civil service learning policies and practices, invested resources, the learning environment, the mandate, governance and capacity and learning outcomes – schools of government are expected to adopt a cohesive and systematic approach to their improvement as public organisations. Like many other public institutions, schools are subject to the same pressures by being asked to do more, do it better, and do it with the same amount of funding or less. Achieving their mandates and supporting the development of competent and professional civil services will require the schools to accelerate their pace of innovation and performance improvement, to modernise their approach to learning and to find new ways of working.

Assessment and recommendations

Schools of government are uniquely positioned to support civil service learning and skills development

- Because of their whole-of-government mandate, schools of government are well positioned to identify the skills and behaviours that are required by all employees, irrespective of their job or function, versus those that are organisationally specific.
- Having in place a learning strategy can make an important contribution to the continued development of the public service in the interest of citizens. More than half of the 2014 OECD Survey of National Schools of Government respondents (16 out of 23 schools) reported having a national learning strategy, with half of them indicating that it applies at both national and sub-national levels of government.
- Most schools of government reported linking national learning strategies to individual employee learning plans, which are also often integrated into the performance management process and used in appointments and promotions in the civil service.
- Most schools of government also noted efforts to align civil service learning programmes with government priorities. Memorandums of understanding and regular discussions with the governments serve as the most frequently used mechanism for alignment. Less than half of the schools (10 out of 24) though reported regular review of their curricula to ensure the continued relevance of their learning programmes.

Schools of government are increasingly innovating in their programmes

- While most survey respondents indicated a preference for traditional classroom training, other teaching methods, such as team-based activities and study tours are increasingly being used (in about 50% of cases). Importantly, while still a minority, approximately 40% of schools of government are providing training to civil servants in the form of online self-study courses. There is also a growing trend of combining several training methods (e.g. executive training may integrate classroom teaching with peer-and in-service learning).
- There seems to be a general alignment between the top-most-ranked learning areas offered by schools of government and the potential skills needs in civil services. Although some disparities exist, people management, information and communication technology (ICT) applications, change management and project management are the areas highly ranked as both learning offerings and skills

needs. At the same time, while risk evaluation, programme evaluation, innovation, stakeholder engagement and policy analysis have been identified among the areas with greatest skills gaps across civil services, learning offerings in these areas generally appear to be scarce.

- Over half of 2014 OECD Survey respondents (18 out of 23) indicated that they are engaged in knowledge development and research, especially applied research and primarily in the areas where schools provide training and development programmes (with the exception of information technology, project management and administrative law).

Further investments are needed to advance monitoring and evaluation for enhanced impact and relevance of schools of government programmes

- Most schools of government have put in place evaluation and monitoring mechanisms for their learning programmes, although most of these are internally managed and carried out using traditional methods. Further investment in independent evaluations and in measuring the impact of training on behavioural changes will be important to ensure ongoing relevance and effectiveness of learning programmes.
- While most of the schools of government report actively evaluating their learning programmes, only 14% of them conducted evaluations of their research activities. As research activities are also subject to demonstrating their value for money, this may also prove to be an area in which schools may need to undertake further investments.

Greater mandate clarity and strengthened institutional framework for learning and development would be beneficial to drive high schools' performance

- While all participating countries reported having in place an institution responsible for civil service learning, they differed in their institutional form, mandate, autonomy and relationship to government and non-governmental stakeholders.
- The internal schools' governance and management models reflect a variety of factors such as the civil service model, schools' legal structures, institutional model (i.e. academic versus public administration), relationships or partnerships with other institutions. While most schools operate under an institutional head, some have also established a board of directors/trustees (20% of respondents) and a council of members (27% of respondents) as the main governance or management bodies to separate the division of duties between day-to-day administration and strategy setting.
- All respondents were established through a form of legal instrument, although further clarity of mandates, roles and responsibilities would be beneficial.

Addressing the challenges, delivering on priorities

- Recognising the importance of learning for effective public sector and the delivery on citizen expectations, schools identify leadership development (in 80% of cases), promoting excellence in government services and policies (47%), alignment of civil service learning activities with the priorities of government (45%) and career development for new public servants (20%) as their priorities.
- Some of the key challenges reported by the schools include limited funding (67%), insufficient qualified human resources (50%), uneven mechanisms for co-ordination with other civil service bodies (40%) and the need to enhance its monitoring and impact evaluation activities. In this context, schools will need to find ways to become more cost-efficient, embrace innovation and modernise their approaches to learning.

Recommendations

- Develop channels to effectively contribute to defining the core competencies required across civil services.
- Support the design and implementation of whole-of-government and organisation-specific civil service learning and development strategies. Where these strategies apply to national and sub-national governments, work with all actors to ensure that the alignment of the learning strategy to the development and delivery of civil service learning programmes.
- Promote the development and use of employee learning plans that take into consideration employee performance and organisational needs.
- Regularly consult with internal and external stakeholders on the identification of civil service skills gaps and learning priorities as part of the process of developing learning programmes.
- Develop the systematic and comprehensive approaches to identify current and emerging government priorities and external trends in order to inform the development of civil service learning and development programmes.
- Regularly review schools' learning and development programmes to ensure that these take into account current and potential future needs and priorities of governments and civil servants.
- Regularly review schools' learning and development programmes to ensure that both the content and delivery methods are best suited to meeting the needs of learners and governments.
- Assess the scope for introducing innovative techniques in the delivery and content of learning and development, including the use of social media and other information and communications technologies.
- Strengthen the link between research and knowledge development activities and learning programmes. This will ensure that learning programmes remain relevant and up to date with changing government priorities and emerging social, economic and political trends.

Recommendations *(continued)*

- Expand the use of comprehensive evaluations of their learning programme effectiveness, with particular attention to the worth, impact, and success of programme outcomes. Particular attention should be given to assessing the impact of learning programmes on employee and organisational effectiveness and performance.
- Consider alternatives to current evaluation methods for the purpose of increasing the breadth, scope and type of programme evaluations. Enhance the use of independent evaluations.
- Consider evaluations of their research and knowledge development activities with particular attention paid to their integration in learning programmes and their impact on institutional and government priorities.
- Ensure clarity of schools' mandates, roles and responsibilities for providing civil service learning and development programmes.
- Strengthen formal means of co-ordination between schools and institutions of national government and, where relevant sub-national governments through the use of a range of co-ordination means and methods. These co-ordination efforts should facilitate the effective communication of priorities and needs as part of the development of a whole-of-government approach to civil service learning and development.
- Develop robust mechanisms to ensure the alignment of learning programmes with the priorities of government in order to address the skills needs associated with learning programme development.
- Consider developing internal governance arrangements, which allow for the input of both governmental and non-governmental stakeholders in order to both ensure responsiveness to government priorities and identify emerging trends and expectations.
- Explore options to provide for greater predictability in the funding models of schools of government in order to fulfil their missions and mandates.
- Consider undertaking schools' capability reviews in order to align human, financial and material resources with the current and future requirements for learning and development, which would meet the needs of current and future civil servants and would support the development of necessary skills.

Chapter 1

Setting the scene: Civil service learning - An evolving priority

This chapter describes main trends challenging governments and testing the resilience and adaptability of public service institutions. The chapter presents some of the concepts and outlines the methodology based on the findings of the 2014 OECD Survey of National Schools of Government, developed by the OECD Global Network of Schools of Government.

Introduction

Policy makers cannot escape today's pressure to respond to economic instability, increasingly complex and ambiguous policy issues, such as global warming, widening inequality and fragile growth prospects in many countries. Addressing these challenges requires an effective and efficient civil service, which is essential for stimulating inclusive economic growth and social welfare. Indeed, OECD studies show that strong institutions, and a strategic capacity and foresight to design and implement reforms and manage risks in the civil service have become vital to improve growth prospects and to react to rapidly occurring and overlapping crises.

At the same time, civil service institutions are challenged like never before by continual change in the economy and society. New technologies, changing economic relations, declining trust in institutions and increasing scepticism, calls for openness, reliance on information and communication technology (ICT) and social media, among other trends, test the resilience and adaptability of public service institutions. Civil service capacity to respond to these factors depends on its ability to:

- identify the skills needed to enable governments to deliver on their priorities and commitments, and address public needs and expectations
- attract and recruit individuals who possess needed skills to civil service, which enables governments to act on their delivery commitments
- develop and nurture individuals' skills through entry and career-long training and development in line with the evolving needs of government
- enable individuals to put to best use their existing and acquired skills for the benefit of civil service and the public (OECD, 2015a).

Achieving these objectives requires developing a learning culture in public service institutions so that employees are encouraged and supported to upgrade their knowledge and skills in response to new government priorities. Investing in employee development through learning is an investment in the institution and an investment in its ability to change and adapt, including:

- **Cultivating capacity to govern**: The capacity of governments to implement policies and programmes benefits from a well-trained and motivated administration, in the absence of which, governments may face difficulties in the implementation of their programmes and priorities.
- **Supporting public administration reform**: The way forward on public administration reform calls for public service staff that are trained to design, implement and monitor reforms and transformation initiatives.
- **Ensuring stability, predictability and adaptability in public administration**: A well-trained public service provides a guarantee and safeguard for the uniform application of administrative rules and regulations, which is important to ensure public confidence in government.
- **Protecting the public interest**: In general terms, a well-trained and motivated public service is important to sustain the securing of core public tasks and the protection of common values (OECD, 1997).

As institutions, schools of government ("schools"'; see Box 1.1 on terminology used throughout this report) are uniquely placed to support civil service learning. They play this role directly through their learning and training programmes, and indirectly, through encouraging a learning culture that contributes to civil service effectiveness and efficiency. However, to remain relevant and responsive to the changing needs of governments and public servants, schools also need to adapt their programming to enable current and future employees to handle the demands of their jobs.

Yet, in most cases, OECD countries are still experiencing the aftermath of the economic crisis, which led in many cases to the reduction in the public financing available for the learning and development of public employees (OECD, 2015a, pp. 72-73). This also underlines the differing capacity of national governments to invest in learning and training programmes (see Chapter 6 for more discussion) and creates a tension between the increasing needs to develop public servants' skills and competencies and declining resources. As such, the schools of government are under increasing pressure to develop new and innovative approaches to learning and development and to enhance their efficiency and effectiveness, while ensuring responsiveness to changing government priorities and needs in skills development.

Box 1.1. Terminology used in this report

For the purposes of this report, unless otherwise indicated, the following terminology has been adopted:

- **Schools of government**, or **schools**, is the generic term used to refer to the institutions that participated in the study. The use of this single generic term should not mask the differences and particularities of these institutions, as there is no one single model for national schools of government.
- **Learning** is the generic term used to describe the process of acquiring new knowledge, skills, or abilities through structured activities. Learning is increasingly an integral part of the process of adaptation to change.
- **Continuous learning** is the generic term used to describe the lifelong process of training, development, and learning.
- **Training and professional development** are the generic terms used to describe the formal process of improving and increasing capabilities of staff in the workplace or through outside organisations. These activities are generically referred to throughout the text as "learning".

Methodology and context

The purpose of this report is to support policy dialogue across OECD and partner countries and economies on the role of schools of government in shaping and supporting the implementation of the governmental agenda, and developing the necessary skills of public servants to respond to government priorities and citizen expectations.

The report is based on the findings of the 2014 OECD Survey of National Schools of Government, developed by the OECD Global Network of Schools of Government (see Box 1.2).

Box 1.2. OECD Global Network of Schools of Government

In response to the growing recognition that an effective and efficient civil service is essential for stimulating economic growth and social welfare, the OECD is increasingly called upon to assist in building civil service capacity to ensure responsiveness to government priorities.

To achieve this objective, the OECD brought together national schools of government in a Global Network of Schools of Government. The network provides direct access to OECD governance expertise and enables exchange of schools' experiences and good practices in ensuring that civil service employees have the skills and competencies to address current and future priorities.

The OECD Global Network of Schools of Government supports countries in securing the long-term sustainability of civil service reforms by:

- strengthening the link between international policy dialogue and national efforts to build capabilities in the civil service
- informing the OECD policy dialogue with lessons and good practices on implementation on the ground
- supporting international exchange among national schools of government and the policy-making community.

The objectives of the OECD Global Network of Schools of Government are to:

- create a professional community of practice by establishing an online OECD platform for information exchange
- facilitate policy dialogue between schools of government and the OECD
- partner current capacity-building and skill-development activities
- monitor research and country-specific activities.

Source: OECD (2015b), "National Schools of Government Network", www.oecd.org/fr/gov/global-network-schools-of-government.htm (accessed 25 July 2016).

The 2014 OECD Survey of National Schools of Government, the first cross-national OECD study of these institutions, contributes to the international comparative knowledge base in this area. The findings are also informed by the discussions that took place at the Third Annual Meeting of the National Schools of Government Network (Paris, 6 July 2015), and are supplemented by a literature review from both academic and practitioner sources (see Box 1.3).

Box 1.3. 2014 OECD Survey of National Schools of Government

Background and purpose

The OECD Survey of National Schools of Government was launched in 2014 as part of the work of the OECD Global Network of Schools of Government. The survey sought to collect comparative information in order to:

- provide comparative benchmarks on the operations, functions and scope of activities of schools of government across OECD and partner countries
- deepen understanding of the role of the schools in implementing and informing government priorities
- inform the activities of the OECD Global Network of Schools of Government.

The survey was distributed by email to all member institutions of the network and was made available via the schools of government platform (www.oecd.org/gov/global-network-schools-of-government.htm). Though the response rate varied by question, the response rate averaged 30% overall (see the list of all 24 respondents in Annex A).

Source: OECD (2014), "2014 OECD Survey of National Schools of Government".

This report was prepared by the Directorate for Public Governance and Territorial Development (GOV) of the Organisation for Economic Co-operation and Development (OECD), within the framework of the activities of the Public Governance Committee.

The report aims to answer the following questions:

- What is learning and why is it important? What is the role of schools of government in promoting civil service learning and developing necessary civil service skills?
- How do schools ensure responsiveness to government priorities in its learning programmes? What evidence base is required in this regard?
- What are the innovative methods used to encourage civil service learning?
- What are the schools' capacities and management models necessary to encourage civil service learning and skills development for responding to government priorities?
- What are the challenges and opportunities that schools of government face in the near term?

The report is structured as follows:

- Chapter 2 looks at the role played by schools of government as institutions that encourage and support civil service learning and skills development, including the presence of national learning and development strategies.
- Chapter 3 considers the teaching and research activities of the schools and the increasing need for schools to innovate in how they deliver their programmes.

- Chapter 4 explores the means by which schools of government evaluate their programmes and their impact on civil services. Considered as part of this discussion are alternatives to current evaluation approaches.
- Chapter 5 considers the institutional foundations of the schools of government and their relationship to government, as well as the means by which schools co-ordinate their activities with other government and non-governmental institutions. Also discussed is the internal governance and management of the schools and how this may influence their mandate and activities.
- Finally, Chapter 6 looks to the issues of the future priorities and challenges that schools of government will be facing in the near term.

References

OECD (2015a), *Government at a Glance 2015*, OECD Publishing, Paris, http://dx.doi.org/10.1787/gov_glance-2015-en.

OECD (2015b), "National Schools of Government Network", www.oecd.org/fr/gov/global-network-schools-of-government.htm (accessed 25 July 2016).

OECD (2014), "2014 OECD Survey of National Schools of Government".

OECD (1997), "Country Pofiles of Civil Service Training Systems", *SIGMA Papers*, No. 12, OECD Publishing, Paris, http://dx.doi.org/10.1787/5kml6g5hxlf6-en.

Chapter 2

Encouraging and supporting civil service learning and skills development

This chapter focuses on the role and responsibilities of schools of government in encouraging and supporting civil service learning and skills development. Developing professionalism in the public service and training and keeping public sector leaders abreast of the competencies that are required for the continuously changing situations and demands is instrumental for achieving national development agendas. In particular, the chapter reviews the ways in which schools determine and respond to the learning needs of civil servants.

Introduction

There is considerable agreement among practitioners and analysts that the current operating context for governments calls for different civil service skills than those required a decade or more ago. As the economic and social contexts in which governments deliver services change, so must governments' investment in staff. At the same time, civil service learning has emerged as one of the key factors contributing to an adaptive, responsive, agile and resilient public service in a period marked by budgetary restraint and the need to establish new and different forms of relationships with citizens. Meeting citizens' expectations in this environment requires investments in public workforces to build capacity to meet these new challenges (OECD, 2015a, p. 3). Schools of government (or "schools") are uniquely placed to play a role in this regard.

When considered from the perspective of the skills required of public servants, OECD, practitioner and academic research converge on the need to develop behavioural attributes (soft skills) and technical attributes (hard skills), such as the ability to challenge the status quo, willingness to innovate, and understanding risk. Skills including leadership, managing the impact of new technologies, the capacity to work with a whole-of-government outlook, and problem solving in complex multidimensional landscapes have been suggested as important to this transformation. In addition, entrepreneurial skills, the ability to be a fixer and facilitator, and capacity to deliver on priorities have also been cited as essential to public service functions, particularly during difficult times (OECD, 2015a; Deloitte, 2015; Dickinson, 2013; Dickinson and Sullivan, 2014; Needham and Mangan, 2015; Medland, 2013).

This chapter focuses on the role and responsibilities of schools of government in encouraging and supporting civil service learning. In particular, the chapter reviews the ways in which schools determine and respond to the learning needs of civil servants.

Civil service learning and development

Employee learning, training and development have become a necessity for most public and private organisations and have attracted high-level attention in recent years. The training and development of civil service employees is vital to any country as it affects the quality of its bureaucracy and policy making (Rajasekar and Khan, 2013). A key building block for civil service learning is the use of competencies to identify needs and develop learning activities that address competency requirements. Across the OECD and partner countries and economies, learning needs are increasingly linked to competency profiles, which tend to define expected behaviours and skills of different groups of public servants, in order to deliver high-quality services and policies to their citizens.

Approaches to civil service learning and development

Two interdependent, though separate, functions enable civil servants to develop the necessary skills and knowledge to respond to internal and external policy pressures and citizen expectations: education and professional development. Whereas education usually provides the foundational knowledge for civil servants at the time of recruitment, training and professional development provide the specific knowledge and skills civil servants will require in a job-specific role (Reichard, 1998). Training and professional development also play a role in the maintenance and upgrading of job-specific skills, knowledge and competencies to encourage continuous learning. Therefore, encouraging continuous workplace learning enables employees and employers to adjust to changes in the environment and meet the challenges that ensue (International Labour Office, 2010). Looking forward, as the needs of civil services changes, activities that enable learning (e.g. training) can also play a major role in ensuring that both new recruits and existing staff possess the skills needed to continue to perform (Dickinson, 2013).

Across OECD and non-OECD countries and economies, learning and training programmes for current and future civil service personnel take two forms: training that takes place within government institutions, such as schools and academies (insourcing); and training that takes place in establishments outside of government, but that are financed by the civil service, for example, through tuition subsidies or institutional maintenance grants (outsourcing). Outsourced training can occur in a variety of settings, such as not-for-profit or private-sector institutions, post-secondary institutions or in academies, institutes and think tanks (OECD, 2015b, p. 210). In addition, a significant number of institutions are hybrids between these two models, meaning that that are both degree-granting higher education institutions and non-degree-granting training and professional development institutions. These institutions address both dimensions of civil service employee development in Reichard's (1998) typology.

Across OECD and non-OECD countries and economies, supporting learning of civil servants is frequently the responsibility of one or more designated national learning and educational bodies, often themselves institutions of the national government. As will be discussed in Chapter 5, though there are many similarities between these institutions, there are also several differences, rooted in factors such as the historical development of national public administrations, different approaches to learning, degrees of integration of new thinking about public administration and the role of management and staff, such as, for example, the adoption of New Public Management (Dobos, 2015, p. 1887).

Therefore, though they each have their own particularities, schools of government in OECD and non-OECD countries and economies share a common focus on civil service learning. While there could be multiple options for encouraging and supporting learning, schools of government tend to be well placed to make a critical and strategic contribution to the development of civil services.

Competencies and skills needed for a well-performing civil service

Competency management has emerged in recent years as one of the leading human resource management (HRM) tools in both the private and public sectors. Competency management has proven effective in defining the abilities and behaviours needed for individuals to be proficient in their jobs. Competency management also enables the linking of skills to HRM activities, thereby ensuring that organisations are staffed with high-performing employees (OECD, 2011). In the context of the needs of national governments, this may include both technical and professional knowledge as well as behavioural requirements, such as leadership.[1]

The importance of knowledge, skills and competencies to individuals and society is widely accepted among policy makers in OECD countries. This applies equally to the general workforce and to the civil service. For employers, whether private or public, investing in competencies marks an investment in human capital and is a key part of an overall recruitment and retention strategy: recruitment to identify the competencies needed of new employees, retention to ensure that these same employees grow with their jobs, and are also prepared for new jobs and challenges.

Indeed, responding to citizen needs and working towards a common purpose, requires agility on the part of civil services, including the capacity to match the numbers, skills, competencies and allocation of the public workforce to new and shifting strategic priorities. This includes identifying and developing capabilities to anticipate and respond to whole-of-government challenges in the civil service. Importantly, there is an ongoing shift towards the increasing importance and emphasis on soft skills necessary for civil servants, which are often seen as different from those of the past. These may include, but are not limited to, interpersonal skills, synthesising skills, organising skills, communications, collaboration and media relations.

Though definitions of competencies vary in the literature, they typically include elements of knowledge, skills and behaviours needed for the effective performance of a given job. While the behavioural aspects may be obtained outside of a formal learning environment, knowledge and skills are often acquired through formal learning activity, either prior to recruitment (i.e. education) or on-the-job training and professional development (Reichard, 1998). One common perspective on competencies is to consider these in terms of core competencies, that is, elements that are deemed essential to successfully perform certain roles. For example, the UK Civil Competency Framework found in Figure 2.1 includes ten competencies arranged in three clusters: setting direction, engaging people and delivering results (Civil Service Human Resources, 2015) (see also Box 2.1).

Figure 2.1. **UK Civil Service Competency Framework 2012-17**

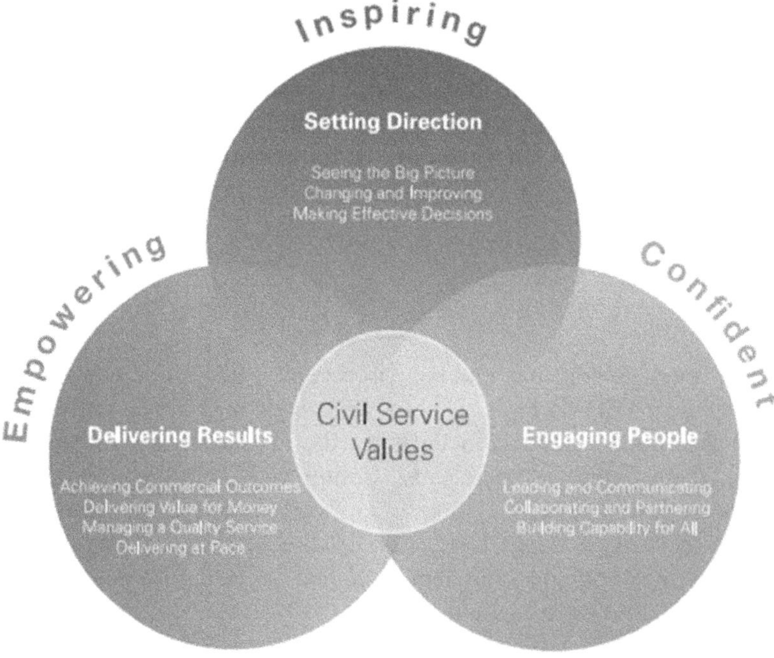

Source: Civil Service Human Resources (2015), "Civil Service Competency Framework 2012-2017", Civil Service Human Resources, London, United Kingdom.

Box 2.1. The United Kingdom's Civil Service Competency Plan

Building skills and competencies

As part of civil service reform, the Government aims to ensure that all civil servants:

- have the tools and skills they need to provide public services more effectively
- can be deployed across departments.

"Meeting the challenge of change: A capabilities plan for the civil service" outlines plans to improve skills and performance across the civil service.

The capability plan includes a strategy for building individuals' skills and competencies, and it examines how the civil service can use structures and management processes to harness these skills.

For example:

- All civil servants are entitled to five days of learning and development each year, targeted to help them perform better in their work.
- There is a wide range of opportunities, such as job shadowing and on-the-job learning, as well as formal training courses.

The plan also encourages more secondments into (and from) the private and voluntary sectors.

Competencies are the skills, knowledge and behaviours that lead to successful performance. The Civil Service Competency Framework sets out how civil servants should work.

Source: Civil Service Human Resources (2015), "Civil Service Competency Framework 2012-2017", Civil Service Human Resources, London, United Kingdom.

In terms of the types of competencies, as shown in Figure 2.2, 80% of respondents (12 out of 15) reported having a set of competencies in place regarding values and ethics in civil service. Yet less than 50% (7 out 15) had established similar competencies for the whole of the civil service or senior management. This finding suggests that job competencies may be more easily defined at a job-specific level than broadly for the whole of the civil service. The exception is values and ethics competencies, which are suitably generic to all job categories and are increasingly seen as a core requirement of civil service employment. This finding is broadly consistent with a previous OECD study that noted the varying national approaches to the integration of competencies into civil service training and development. Whereas some competency profiles are narrow and specific, others can be generic to a broad range of government jobs (OECD, 2011, pp. 128-130).

Figure 2.2. **The development of civil service competencies in national schools of government**

Q. Has your government developed a set of competencies?

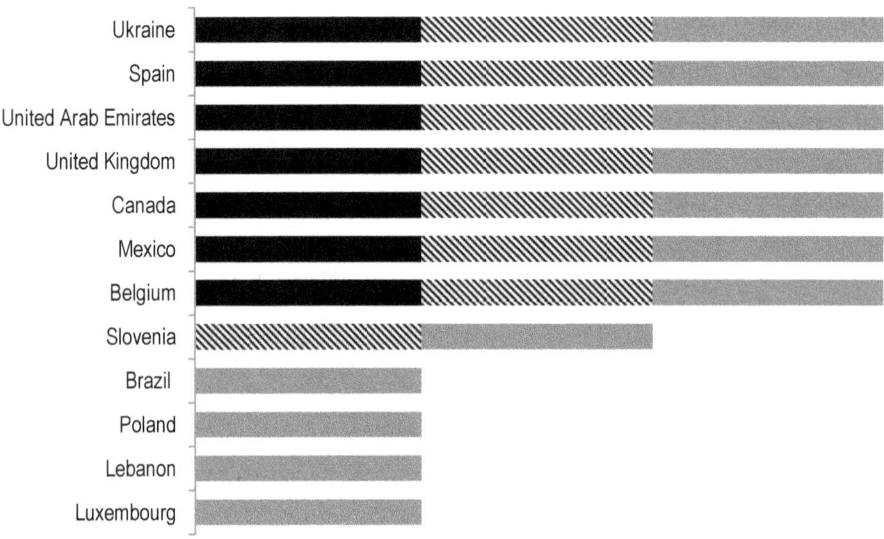

Source: OECD (2014b), "2014 OECD Survey of National Schools of Government".

For senior civil servants, most OECD countries develop a centrally defined skills profile that tends to be common across senior civil service. The priority competencies are strongly related to the capacity to manage teams, networks and change; the ability to think strategically and give policy advice; and adhere to values and ethics (OECD, 2016; see Figure 2.3). The competency approach emphasises that while some leadership characteristics may be innate, many aspects of leadership can be learned (see Box 2.2).

Figure 2.3. **Priority competencies for senior managers**

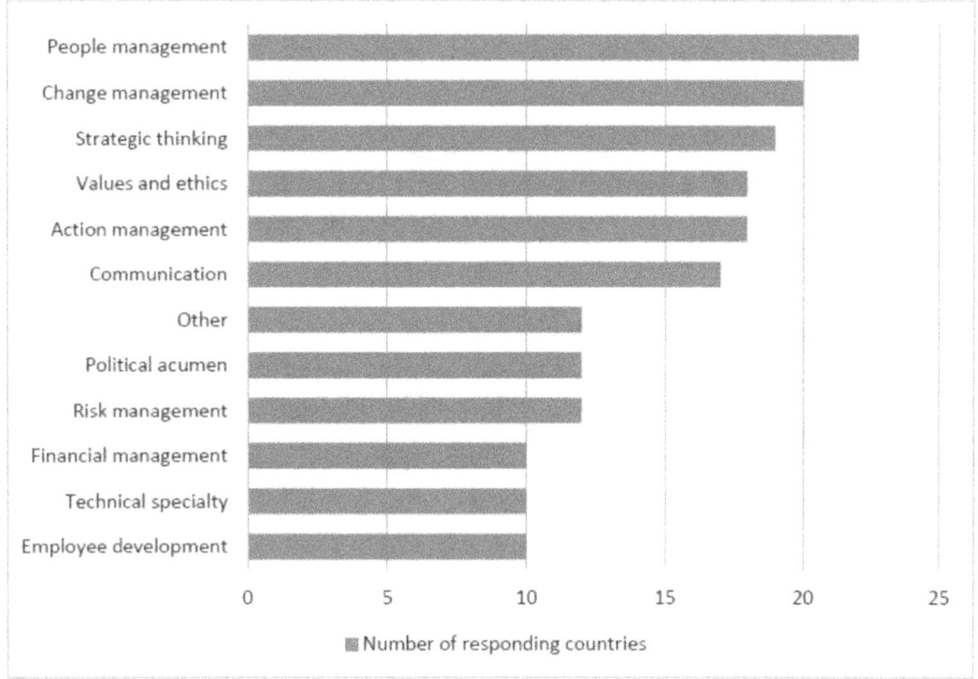

Source: OECD (2016), "Strategic Human Resources Management Survey".

Box 2.2. **The new Key Leadership Competencies in Canada**

The Key Leadership Competencies define the behaviours expected of leaders in Canada's public service. These leaders play a pivotal role in creating and sustaining a modern, connected and high-performing public service that is ethical, professional and non-partisan.

This competency profile serves as the basis for selection, learning and development, performance and talent management of executives and other senior leaders.

Create vision and strategy

Leaders define the future and chart a path forward. They are adept at understanding and communicating context, factoring in the economic, social and political environment. Intellectually agile, they leverage their deep and broad knowledge, build on diverse ideas and perspectives and create consensus around compelling visions. Leaders balance organisational and government-wide priorities and improve outcomes for Canada and Canadians.

Mobilise people

Leaders inspire and motivate the people they lead. They manage performance, provide constructive and respectful feedback to encourage and enable performance excellence. They lead by example, setting goals for themselves that are more demanding than those that they set for others.

Box 2.2. **The new Key Leadership Competencies in Canada** *(continued)*

Uphold integrity and respect

Leaders exemplify ethical practices, professionalism and personal integrity. They create respectful and trusting work environments where sound advice is valued. They encourage the expression of diverse opinions and perspectives, while fostering collegiality. Leaders are self-aware and seek out opportunities for personal growth.

Collaborate with partners and stakeholders

Leaders are deliberate and resourceful about seeking the widest possible spectrum of perspectives. They demonstrate openness and flexibility to forge consensus and improve outcomes. They bring a whole-of-government perspective to their interactions. In negotiating solutions, they are open to alternatives and skilful at managing expectations. Leaders share recognition with their teams and partners.

Promote innovation and guide change

Leaders have the courage and resilience to challenge convention. They create an environment that supports bold thinking, experimentation and intelligent risk taking. They use setbacks as a valuable source of insight and learning. Leaders take change in their stride, aligning and adjusting milestones and targets to maintain forward momentum.

Achieve results

Leaders mobilise and manage resources to deliver on the priorities of the Government, improve outcomes and add value. They consider context, risks and business intelligence to support high-quality and timely decisions. They anticipate, plan, monitor progress and adjust as needed. Leaders take personal responsibility for their actions and the outcomes of their decisions.

Source: Treasury Board Secretariat (2016), "Key Leadership Competency profile and examples of effective and ineffective behaviours", Treasury Board Secretariat, Government of Canada, www.tbs-sct.gc.ca/psm-fpfm/learning-apprentissage/pdps-ppfp/klc-ccl/klcp-pccl-eng.asp.

The 2014 OECD Survey of National Schools of Government (or "OECD Survey") also reveals that where competency sets may not exist at the national government level, these may exist at the level of individual governmental institutions, e.g. departments, ministries or agencies. In this regard 56% of respondents (5 out of 9 respondents to this question) indicated that the development of organisational learning plans resides at the level of individual institutions. In such cases, the development of competency sets would reflect the specific functions of staff in relation to the mandate of the institution. For example, the competencies required for an economist in an economics department may vary from those required in a science-based or social-policy-oriented department. Furthermore, these differences may also highlight the organisation of the national governments and the authorities assigned to these institutions for human resource management.

Overall, the findings shown in Figures 2.4 and 2.5 further in this chapter suggest that countries accord greater attention to the development of competencies in areas marked by behavioural skills requirements rather than technical skills. This preference may stem from the large number of professional and technical occupations in national civil services that would make the development of competencies based on technical skills costly and impractical.

The role of schools of government in developing civil service skills and competencies

One consequence of the application of competency management in public administrations has been the greater emphasis placed on "upskilling their workforce, continuing professional development and lifelong learning" (OECD, 2011, p. 125). The development of changing competencies also requires new types of training and development approaches. As national institutions with the mandate to provide learning, training and professional development to civil servants, schools play an important role in civil service skills and knowledge development. In fact, acquired competencies are often seen as learning outcomes in terms of knowledge, skills and abilities of schools' activities and become an important issue in evaluation of schools' performance. In this capacity, schools complement learning and development that occurs as part of workplace activities, and supplement knowledge acquired as part of other formal secondary and post-secondary education and professional development. Schools are engaged in an array of activities that contribute to civil service development. In particular, the findings presented in Figure 2.4 show the areas of primary responsibility of schools. The results show that schools are principally involved in activities that are related to training and professional development activities, such as organising conferences (79% or 19 out of 24 respondents to this question); integrity and values training (75% or 18 out of 24 respondents to this question); and management and leadership development (75% or 18 out of 24 respondents and 70% or 17 out of 24 respondents to this question, respectively). In addition, they are also responsible for maintaining international partnerships (66% or 16 out of 24 respondents to this question) and providing advisory services to government (60% or 14 out of 24 respondents to this question). Schools are also active in areas best described as contributing to the role of government as a whole, such as promoting public service innovation (75% or 18 out of 24 respondents to this question); dissemination of good practices (58% or 14 out of 24 respondents to this question); and knowledge development through their applied and academic research activities (41% or 10 out of 24 respondents and 29% or 7 out of 24 respondents to this question, respectively). However, these activities are extensions or adjuncts to the role of schools in training and development (see Box 2.3).

Figure 2.4. **Responsibilities of national schools of government**

Q. What are the primary responsibilities of the school (national government level)?

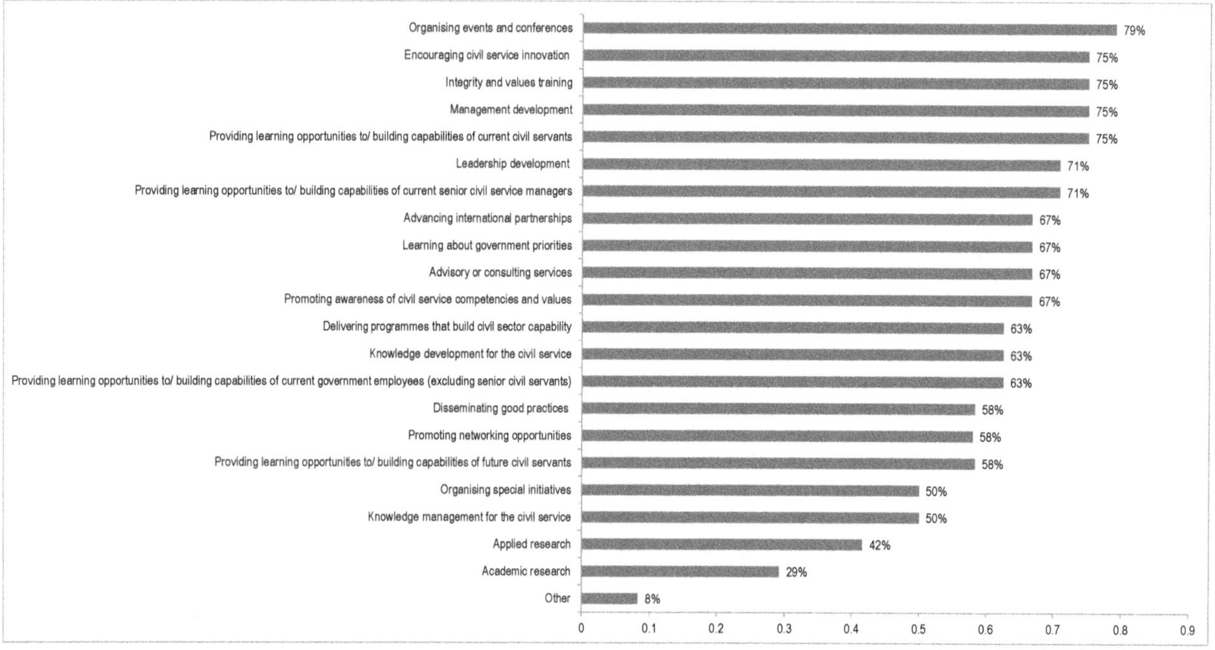

Responsibility	Share
Organising events and conferences	79%
Encouraging civil service innovation	75%
Integrity and values training	75%
Management development	75%
Providing learning opportunities to/ building capabilities of current civil servants	75%
Leadership development	71%
Providing learning opportunities to/ building capabilities of current senior civil service managers	71%
Advancing international partnerships	67%
Learning about government priorities	67%
Advisory or consulting services	67%
Promoting awareness of civil service competencies and values	67%
Delivering programmes that build civil sector capability	63%
Knowledge development for the civil service	63%
Providing learning opportunities to/ building capabilities of current government employees (excluding senior civil servants)	63%
Disseminating good practices	58%
Promoting networking opportunities	58%
Providing learning opportunities to/ building capabilities of future civil servants	58%
Organising special initiatives	50%
Knowledge management for the civil service	50%
Applied research	42%
Academic research	29%
Other	8%

Source: OECD (2014b), "2014 OECD Survey of National Schools of Government".

Box 2.3. **National schools of government: Missions and mandates**

Colombia's Superior School of Public Administration

To educate citizens in the knowledge, values and skills that are used in the public administrative field for the development of society and the State and for the enhancement of management capacity of entities and organisations that provide public service, at the different levels of higher education, education for work and human development, research and technical assistance in regional, national and global contexts. (See www.esap.edu.co/portal/index.php/what-is-esap/.)

Latvian School of Public Administration

(…) The LSPA provides a high-quality training and consultation service to meet the current and future needs of public administration and municipalities. The training and services developed by the LSPA help further to ensure high quality of public service in Latvia.

The LSPA is the largest training centre for civil servants and public administration employees in Latvia. The LSPA develops open and tailor-made training for both the public and private sectors, and oversees the certification of internal audit specialists in public service. (See www.vas.gov.lv/en/.)

Spain's National Institute of Public Administration (INAP)

While the main tasks of the INAP have traditionally been the training and improvement of the civil service, nowadays it performs a wide array of activities that may be classified in the following areas: 1) recruitment into the civil service; 2) training and professional improvement of public employees; 3) research and publishing; and 4) international relations. In addition, the Institute carries out a wide variety of educational and academic activities, intergovernmental co-operation and the analysis of public policies through conferences, meetings and seminars.

Box 2.3. **National schools of government: Missions and mandates** *(continued)*

United Arab Emirates' Mohammed Bin Rashid School of Government

(…) By preparing, qualifying and empowering tomorrow's leaders, and by strengthening government capacity in the United Arab Emirates and the Arab world, our school aims to promote effective public policy through focusing on applied research and engaging the public and private sectors in the development process. (See www.mbrsg.ae/HOME/ABOUT-US/President-s-Welcome.aspx.)

Responsibilities of the President of the Canada School of Public Service

6.2. The President of the Canada School of Public Service is responsible for:

- developing and regularly updating, in collaboration with the relevant policy authorities, courses and programmes that meet the Standards on Knowledge for Required Training, and for delivering these courses and programmes and assessing whether participants successfully complete them
- supporting deputy heads in their efforts to strengthen organisational leadership, apply leading-edge management practices and promote innovation
- developing measures and standards against which to assess its programmes and performance relative to this policy.

6.2.1. In relation to Required Training, responsibilities of the President of the Canada School of Public Service include design and delivery of:

- orientation programmes for new employees of the core public administration
- courses and programmes for first-time managers at all levels
- courses and programmes for functional specialists in areas defined by the employer
- instruments for assessing knowledge for existing managers, executives and functional specialists in areas defined by the employer.

6.2.2. In relation to Leadership Development Programmes, responsibilities of the President of the Canada School of Public Service include developing, delivering and regularly updating the educational component of the corporate leadership development programmes to effectively meet the evolving needs of these programmes.

6.2.3. In relation to Professional Development, responsibilities of the President of the Canada School of Public Service include providing opportunities for and supporting the professional development of employees at all levels. (See www.tbs-sct.gc.ca/pol/doc-eng.aspx?id=12405.)

Source: Author, based on publicly available sources.

Examples of different national approaches to civil service competency development are provided in Box 2.4; they are based on examples provided at the 2016 National Schools of Government Network Annual Meeting (OECD, forthcoming).

Box 2.4. Examples of national approaches to civil service competency development

Hungary

The National University of Public Service (NUPS) has been providing training programmes that are based on the assessment of civil service competencies. Competency and skills mapping are an integral part of NUPS' approach to the development of training programmes. NUPS sees its role as helping public institutions acquire a learning culture, and to encourage civil servants to seek to continually improve. Encouraging civil servants to innovate is one of the main elements of this approach. To support its activities NUPS makes use of digital government tools such as consultations, e-learning and tutorials.

Kazakhstan

The Academy of Public Administration of Kazakhstan (APA) plays an important role in the modernisation of the country's civil service and is Kazakhstan's only civil service training organisation. The Academy provides training to civil servants based on competency profiles that have developed to reflect the needs and realities of different levels within the civil service. These profiles are used to assess the competencies of civil servants at the beginning of their training and can therefore be used to tailor training to their needs. The Academy also places great importance in international co-operation with leading schools of government around the world as examples of good practice.

Latvia

The training offered by the School of Public Administration was developed to closely match needs derived from the governmental agenda. The school's programmes reflect governmental priorities, thereby ensuring that civil service learning is relevant to the operating context. The training provided by the school focuses principally on competency development, such as coaching for managers and is offered by practitioners who are themselves civil servants. In the future, Latvia's School of Public Administration is looking for opportunities to develop joint training programmes and partnerships between schools of government in order to leverage the expertise of several institutions in its training programmes, such as in the area of change management.

Philippines

The Development Academy of the Philippines was established to maintain a quality bureaucracy that exemplifies competence, integrity and commitment to public service. The Academy contributes to the development of public leaders who adhere to the same values and who possess a deep sense of mission to upgrade the life of every Filipino. In 2012, the Academy established the National Government Career Executive Service Development Programme with the goal of fostering career advancement in government and promoting stability in the bureaucracy by producing a corps of development-oriented, competent, dedicated, and honest high-level civil servants (senior executives and middle managers).

Source: OECD (forthcoming), "National Schools of Government Network Annual Meeting 2016: Summary report", OECD.

Taken together, these findings highlight the complex nature of the role of schools in skills and competency development. This can be partly explained by the diversity of the schools that responded to the OECD Survey and the differences in their roles and mandates. This was observed by several stakeholders, who noted that the attention focused on skills and competency development will vary between schools with post-recruitment training roles versus those engaged in post-graduate education (OECD, forthcoming).

A key issue in the development of a professional civil service is the identification of the skills that are important for civil services - and the existing skills gaps. Figure 2.5 shows a relative discrepancy between the areas with the greatest skills gaps and those areas where schools provide the greatest learning and skills development opportunities. However, it also shows that the top five civil service skills gaps identified by respondents (people management; information management and the application of new technologies; change management; risk evaluation; and regulatory quality) are all among the most provided learning and development opportunities.

Figure 2.5. **Civil service skills gaps and learning and development opportunities**

Q. Please provide information on the areas in which your school provides learning and development opportunities. Please also indicate if any are skills lacking in the civil service.

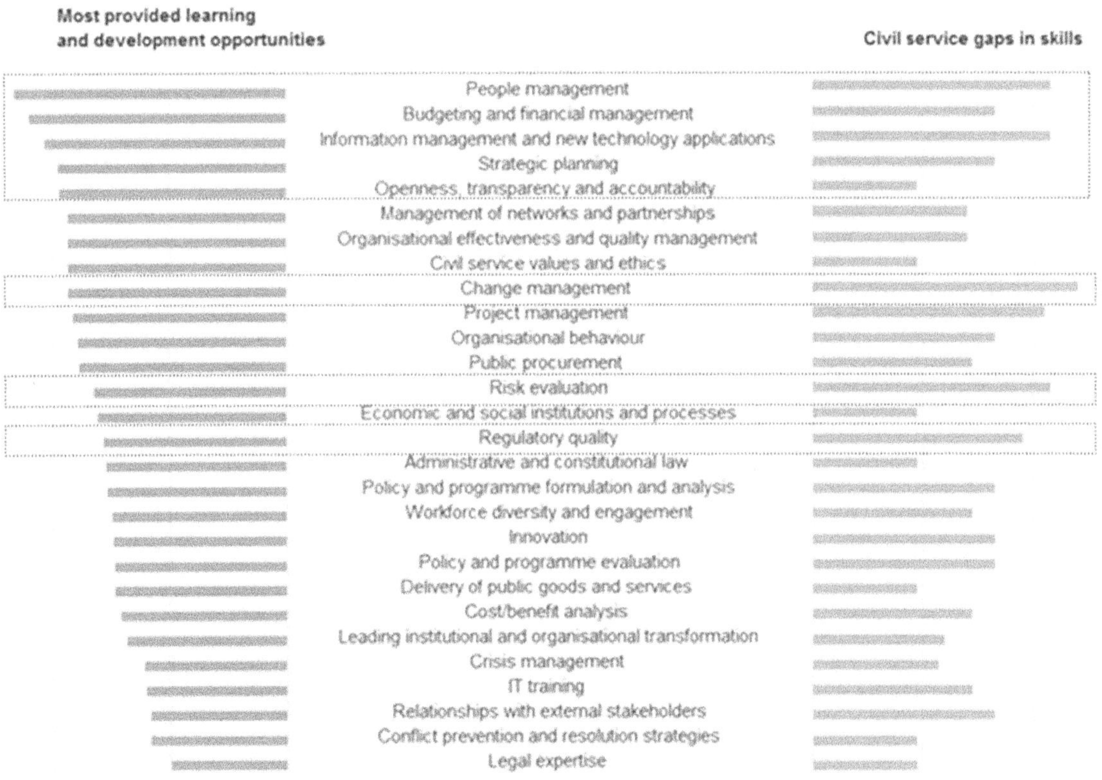

Most provided learning and development opportunities
Civil service gaps in skills

People management
Budgeting and financial management
Information management and new technology applications
Strategic planning
Openness, transparency and accountability
Management of networks and partnerships
Organisational effectiveness and quality management
Civil service values and ethics
Change management
Project management
Organisational behaviour
Public procurement
Risk evaluation
Economic and social institutions and processes
Regulatory quality
Administrative and constitutional law
Policy and programme formulation and analysis
Workforce diversity and engagement
Innovation
Policy and programme evaluation
Delivery of public goods and services
Cost/benefit analysis
Leading institutional and organisational transformation
Crisis management
IT training
Relationships with external stakeholders
Conflict prevention and resolution strategies
Legal expertise

Source: OECD (2014b), "2014 OECD Survey of National Schools of Government".

The OECD Survey also reveals the degree of involvement of schools in assessing civil service competencies. One such area is leadership. As shown in Figure 2.6, over half of the respondents reported their involvement in the assessment of staff leadership competencies. Leadership competency development approaches in OECD countries range from special development programmes, executive leadership training, training for middle management and having a whole-of-government training approach.

Figure 2.6. **The degree of involvement of national schools of government in assessing leadership competencies**

Q. Does the school play a role in assessing leadership competencies of executives and identifying areas of improvement?

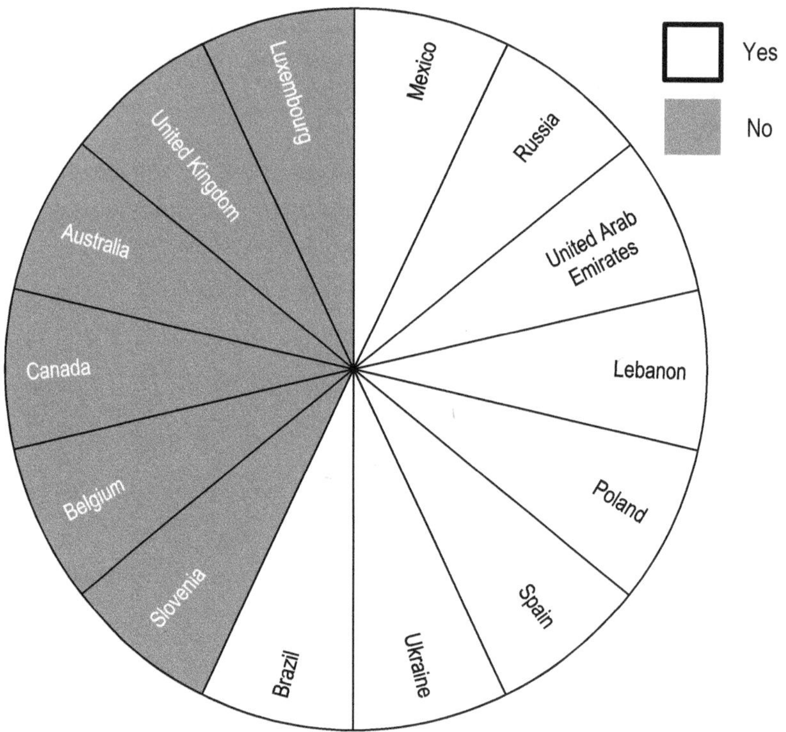

Source: OECD (2014b), “2014 OECD Survey of National Schools of Government”.

National civil service learning and development strategies

While there could be multiple training and development opportunities, schools play an important role in ensuring the capacity of civil services to deliver on the government agenda and respond to citizen expectations. One indicator of the importance accorded to employee learning and professional development is found in the presence of a national strategy that institutionalises a country’s commitment to civil service learning. This can take several forms, including legislation, administrative policies or practice guidelines. National civil service learning strategies serve to enshrine the commitment to learning as well as to encapsulate how learning and professional development contribute to the achievement of organisational goals and objectives as well as fulfil individual needs. The existence of a learning strategy also serves as a means of ensuring the accountability of governments to learning and development[2] and provides the means and indicators for assessing performance in this area (United Nations Public Administration Network, n.d.).

Having a learning strategy in place can make an important contribution to the continued development of the civil service in the interest of citizens. As discussed above, though the civil service shares many characteristics with other sectors of the economy, it is also sufficiently different to warrant an approach to learning that recognises the different specific drivers and factors that come from its public mission. Though learning strategies are by nature context specific, reflecting needs, resources, and capacities that are present, some common elements may include:

- identification of the tools and support needed by civil services to deliver
- forward-thinking plans to support the learning and development needs of employees
- identification of current and future learning trends, including consideration of new learning methods (such as e-learning) that may substitute for, or complement, traditional learning approaches, such as classroom learning
- consideration of organisational roles in supporting access to learning, and the impact of new and emerging technologies and tools
- consideration of social and economic factors that have an impact on learning, such as increasing workforce and community diversity and the need to provide inclusive approaches to learning
- consideration of the responsibility of individuals in learning (Government of British Columbia, n.d.).[3]

Some 60% of respondents to the OECD Survey (16 out of 23 respondents to this question) reported having a national learning strategy (see Figure 2.7). However, the form and content of these national strategies differ depending on the model of civil service. Two examples of national learning strategies are provided in Box 2.5 (Treasury Board Secretariat, 2008; Civil Service Training and Development, 2011). Countries with an open position-based system tend to put more emphasis on specific position-related training. This is in line with an approach to recruitment that provides for a more diverse set of candidates with less of a common culture and varying knowledge about government affairs and procedures. By contrast, for mainly career-based systems, new recruits to the civil service are mainly selected after university graduation or early in their careers. In this approach, more emphasis is placed on early training and less is on lifelong learning.

Figure 2.7. **The presence of national civil service learning and development strategies in schools of government**

Q. Have a civil service learning/training strategy and action plan been developed?

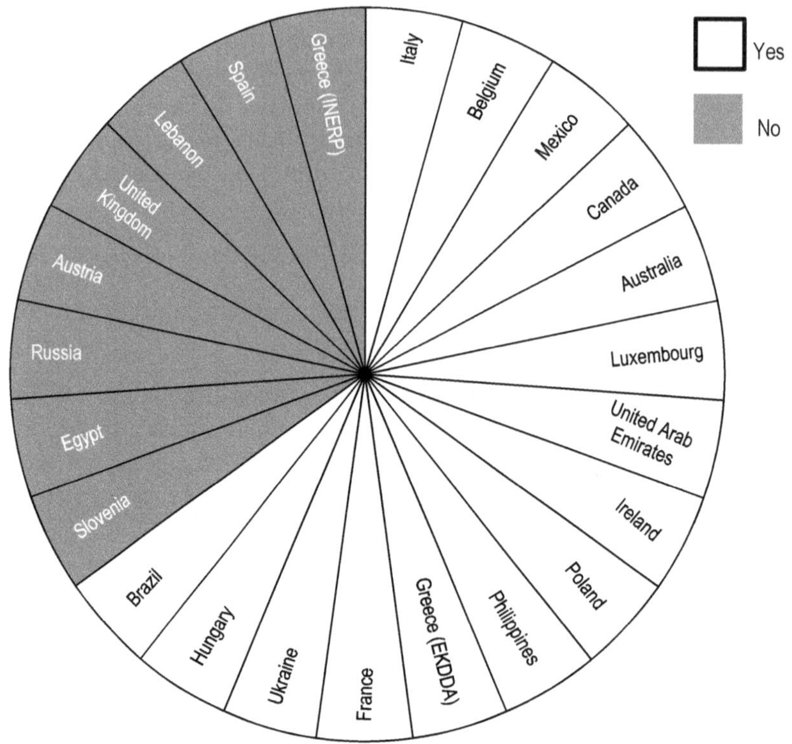

Source: OECD (2014b), "2014 OECD Survey of National Schools of Government".

Box 2.5. **National civil service learning strategies in Canada and Ireland**

Canada: Policy on Learning, Training, and Development

The objective of this policy is to help build a skilled, well-trained and professional workforce; to strengthen organisational leadership; and to adopt leading-edge management practices to encourage innovation and continuous improvements in performance.

The expected results of this policy are that:

- New employees will share a common understanding of their role as public servants.
- Managers at all levels will have the necessary knowledge to effectively exercise their delegated authorities.
- Specialists in finance, human resources, internal audit, procurement, materiel management, real property, information management, and other domains as may be specified, will meet professional standards established by the employer.
- Participants enrolled in corporate leadership development programmes will help meet the current and future human resources needs of the core public administration.

Box 2.5. **National civil service learning strategies in Canada and Ireland** *(continued)*

- Employees at all levels will acquire and maintain the knowledge, skills and competencies related to their level and functions.
- Senior public service leaders will align learning with the management improvement objectives of government and departmental business priorities.
- Leading-edge practices in civil service management will be applied to encourage innovation and continuous improvements in performance.

Ireland: Learning and Development Framework for the Civil Service 2011-14

This Framework is a high-level document focusing on the key learning and development (L&D) objectives that should be pursued by the civil service within the next four years. It is anticipated that this will be a period of considerable change and challenge for all departments. Due to the divergent nature of the organisations that make up the civil service, not every organisation can implement this Framework at the same pace.

This Framework is designed to reflect the key L&D objectives that arise for the various organisations over the lifetime of the Framework, as set out below:

1. prioritise business needs and align business, human resources and learning strategies
2. analyse L&D needs
3. develop strategies for addressing L&D needs
4. evaluate L&D
5. strengthen ethics and governance
6. promote strong financial management.

The stages of the training cycle, as reflected in the objectives of this policy, are to help build a skilled, well-trained and professional workforce; to strengthen organisational leadership; and to adopt leading-edge management practices to encourage innovation and continuous improvements in performance.

Source: OECD (2014b), "2014 OECD Survey of National Schools of Government"; Treasury Board Secretariat (2008), "Policy on Learning, Training and Development", Treasury Board Secretariat, Canada, www.tbs-sct.gc.ca/pol/doc-eng.aspx?id=12405; Civil Service Training and Development (2011), "Learning and Development Framework for the Civil Service, 2011-2014", Civil Service Training and Development, Ireland, http://hr.per.gov.ie/wp-content/uploads/2011/04/Learning-and-Development-Framework.pdf.

The areas of application of the learning strategies are also relevant. Approximately 60% of respondents to the OECD Survey (8 out of 15 respondents to this question) noted that their national civil service learning applied at both the national and sub-national levels of government (see Figure 2.8). These responses are broadly in line with the systems of government in the respondents' countries. The OECD Survey also highlights a dimension where intergovernmental agreements or other vehicles permit collaboration across levels of government in the area of civil service learning. In a context where the goal may be to establish a common learning framework, the ability to plan learning strategies across levels of government would increase the impact of reaching such a goal.

Figure 2.8. **Level of government covered by national schools of government civil service learning strategies**

Q. Please select all levels of government covered by the strategy and action plans

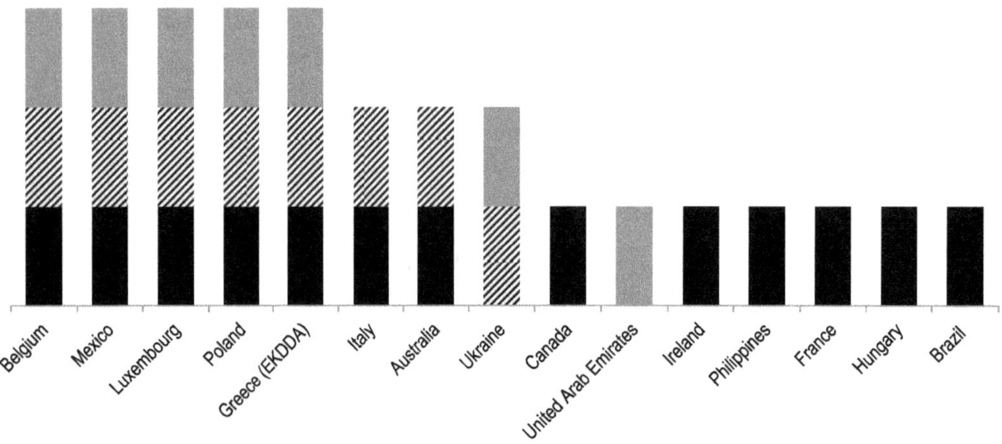

Source: OECD (2014b), "2014 OECD Survey of National Schools of Government".

While the existence of national learning strategies is a positive step, it is also important to consider how they are implemented. Principally, by having in place learning strategies, governments are able to anchor their approach to civil service learning and development within a broader whole-of-government function rather than have training defined by silos determined by departmental or ministry divisions (Dickinson, 2013). It is therefore interesting to note that only four countries reported having a national learning strategy that applied horizontally (across government) and vertically (within individual ministries): Brazil, Mexico, Poland and the United Arab Emirates. For example, in Brazil each ministry or agency of the government is responsible for developing a training plan that aligns with the human resources guidelines issued by the central government. This practice enables the alignment of departmental learning plans to broader government-wide objectives and, consequently, contributes to ensuring a uniform approach to civil service development. In addition, while providing for a degree of uniformity to training, linking organisational learning strategies to the learning strategy at the national level is also consistent with a career-based approach to civil service training, by fostering mobility across governmental bodies over the span of a career.

Another element to be considered is the degree to which individual employee learning plans are linked to the civil service learning strategies. This practice is followed by all of the survey respondents and, consequently, could be viewed as good practice. Other uses for such strategies include integration of learning strategies into the performance management process (67% or 6 out of 9 respondents do so; see Figure 2.9) and its use in appointments and promotions (89% or 8 out of 9 respondents do so).

Figure 2.9. **Link between civil service learning strategies and performance management in national schools of government**

Q. Is there a link between the learning strategy and performance management process?

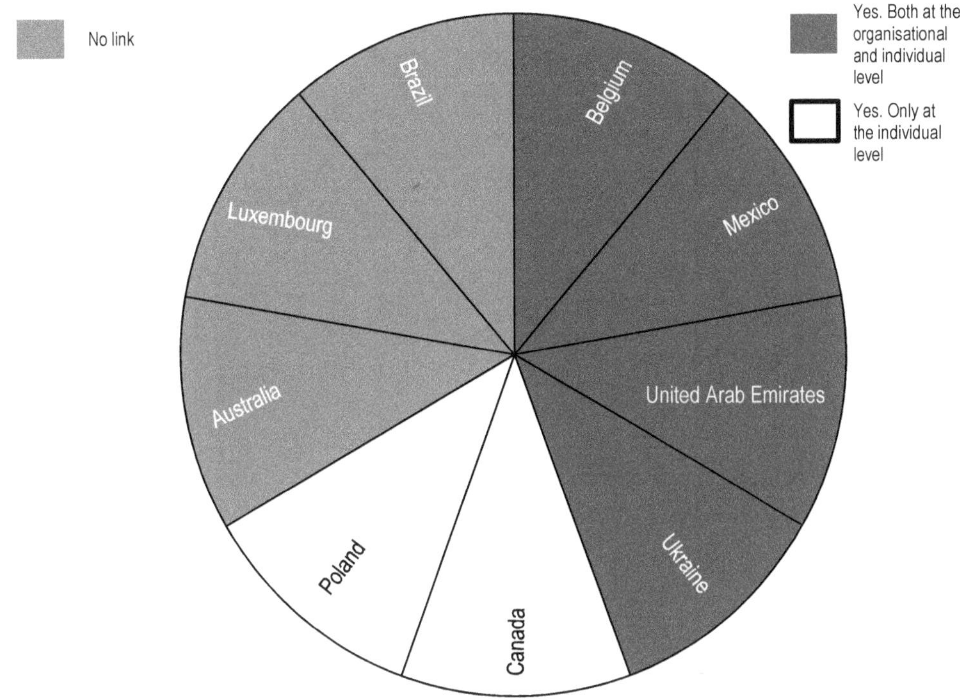

Source: OECD (2014b), "2014 OECD Survey of National Schools of Government".

By contrast, the alignment of learning strategies to overall government priorities varies considerably among respondents. This may be explained by the differences stemming from the forms of government as well as the role and place of the schools of government. However, most respondents noted the objective of ensuring the continued development of civil service capacities. In some instances, the strategies also went beyond learning and development and considered the overall contribution of the schools in areas such as research (e.g. Ukraine) or support for good governance as a general objective of government (e.g. United Arab Emirates).

Another factor which needs to be considered is the degree to which civil service learning strategies can address the learning needs of all civil service staff in detail. For example, certain professions may have their own requirements for professional development or continuing education. In such instances public administration need to comply with these requirements in order to maintain the professional credentials of their personnel, especially if their professional designation is inherent to their duties.[4] Therefore, public administrations also need to account for these requirements as part of their overall training and professional development policies. It follows that learning strategies should encapsulate a commitment to learning, rather than attempt to be a comprehensive listing of all possible learning needs and requirements (see Figure 2.10).

Figure 2.10. **Presence of organisational civil service learning plans in national schools of government**

Q. Does each public organisation have an organisational learning plan?

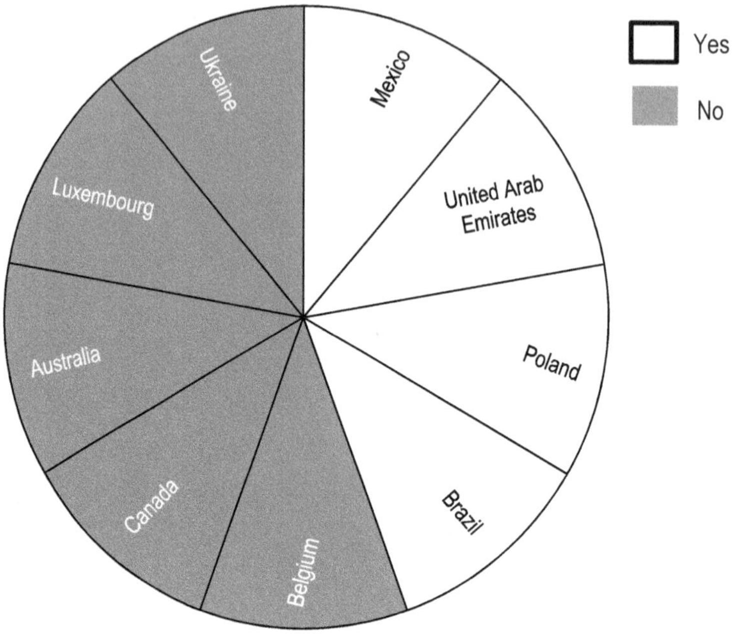

Yes: Mexico, United Arab Emirates, Poland, Brazil

No: Belgium, Canada, Australia, Luxembourg, Ukraine

Source: OECD (2014b), "2014 OECD Survey of National Schools of Government".

Identification of civil service learning and development needs

Evolving employee tasks and technological advances also require employees to continually upgrade or update their skills and knowledge. The same can be said of processes aimed at identifying and supporting particular employees in their career progression through a talent management approach. All of these elements fit within a strategy to identify gaps in skills, knowledge and capacity building.

As Figure 2.11 highlights, nearly all respondents to the OECD Survey have made an ongoing review of employee training and development needs a feature of their approach to human resource management. This approach ensures that employees can be proficient in their jobs, are adaptable to changing needs and, possibly, prepared for further challenges through a job change or promotion. In addition, in the cases of Belgium, Canada, Mexico, Poland, Ukraine and the United Arab Emirates, this assessment was also part of the performance management process, be it at the level of individual employees or at the level of the organisation.

Figure 2.11. **The presence of an ongoing review of civil service training and development needs in national schools of government**

Q. Does the strategy require the continuing regular review of the training and development needs of employees throughout their employment?

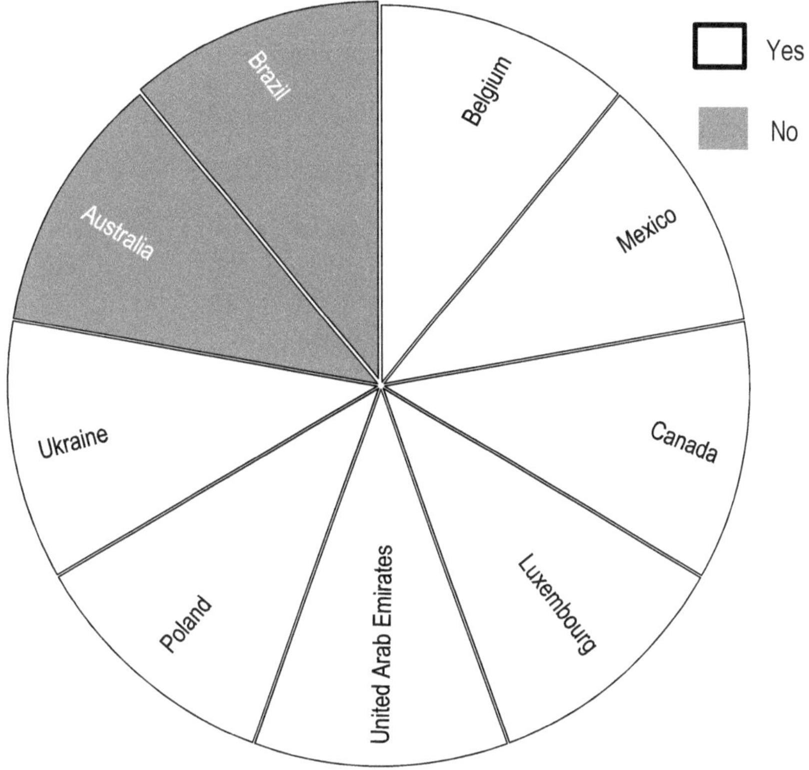

Source: OECD (2014b), "2014 OECD Survey of National Schools of Government".

Schools of government can be seen as an interface between the national government as an institution - and its employees, who implement its priorities and commitments. This gives national schools of government an opportunity to act in both a capacity-building role and as agents of change. In doing so, they can bring to the civil service the ability to learn about, and integrate, new ideas and innovations consistent with its mission. However, the ability of these institutions to undertake these roles depends in large part on their ability to integrate the priorities of the national government into its programming. It also reflects the importance that the national government places on civil service training and professional development.

In addition, as shown in Figure 2.12, schools largely tend to base the development of their learning programmes on informal inputs in meetings with either their national sponsoring institution (i.e. a central governmental institution), its objective clientele (departments and ministries), or self-directed efforts to identify priorities from statements of government priorities. Though less frequently cited, 8 schools also include advisory bodies in the process of shaping learning programmes. For example the governance structure of the Regional School of Public Administration (ReSPA) includes an advisory board which provides input into the development of its programming (ReSPA, 2008). The reliance on horizontal scans, reviews of academic literature and other means is rare, however.

Figure 2.12. **Channels for the identification of civil service training and development priorities in national schools of government**

Q. What are the principal channels through which the school identifies its training and development focus areas?

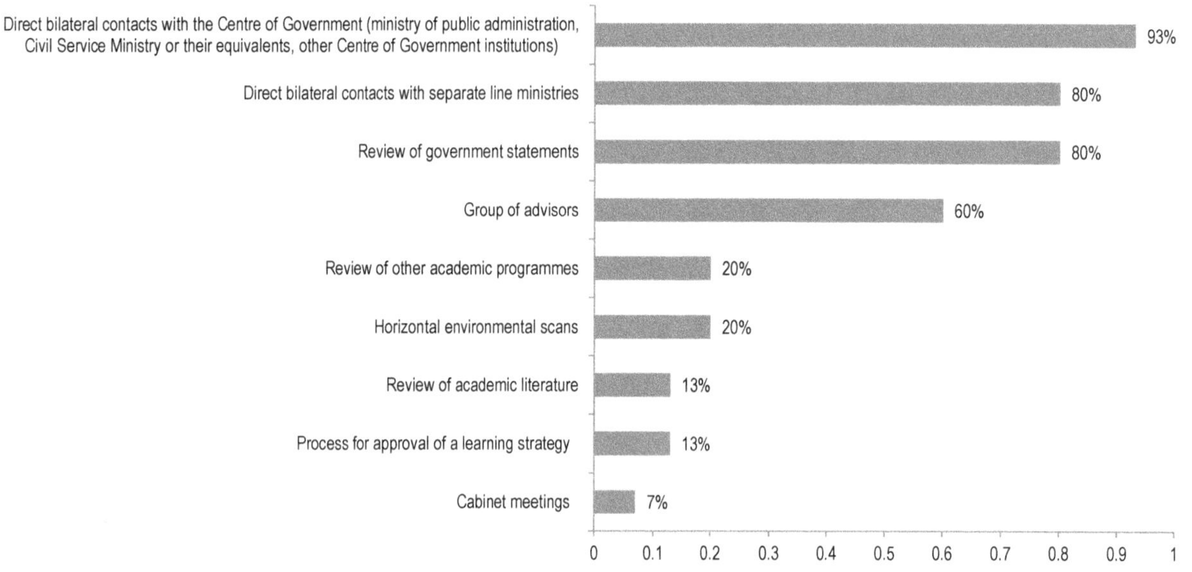

Source: OECD (2014b), "2014 OECD Survey of National Schools of Government".

Overall, these results suggest that it is either the senior ranks of civil service or human resources (HR) services that identify civil service skills needs. Their contributions stem from the respective understanding of overall governmental priorities and strategic workforce planning. By contrast, few survey respondents referred to the use of surveys or engagement with internal or external stakeholders in the process of assessing the knowledge needs of civil servants. Where survey-type instruments have been used, this tends to involve only staff within a single ministry or agency rather than government-wide. This appears to suggest that there may to be greater emphasis placed on competencies defined at the narrower institutional end rather than the broader government-wide perspective. Therefore, the identification of civil service skills needs and gaps are often identified and included in a learning curriculum by proxy, such as through senior managers. Although there is an assessment of skills and knowledge, it appears to be restricted to a small cadre of individuals and functions, with a broad array of inputs, such as from stakeholders external to government or international experiences, playing a limited role.

Identification of civil service knowledge needs

The operating context for governments across the globe is steadily evolving and, as a consequence, so must the approach to, and content of, training and professional development of civil service staff at all levels. As noted above, maintaining and upgrading technical knowledge and skills is one important element, but another is ensuring that staff possess the necessary behavioural and other skills to be proficient in their jobs. As shown in Figure 2.13, the determination of civil service knowledge needs is based on a variety of means according to respondents to the OECD Survey. These include:

- regular discussions with HR services across the civil service
- regular discussions with senior management across the civil service.

These are followed by:

- assessments of government programmes and priorities
- regular engagement with other stakeholders
- performance evaluations.

The least-used methods include:

- horizon scanning
- civil service employee surveys conducted by the centre of government (CoG)
- surveys of external stakeholders conducted by the government
- surveys of external stakeholders conducted by the school.

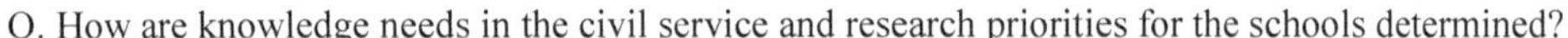

Figure 2.13. **Determination of civil service knowledge needs in national schools of government**

Q. How are knowledge needs in the civil service and research priorities for the schools determined?

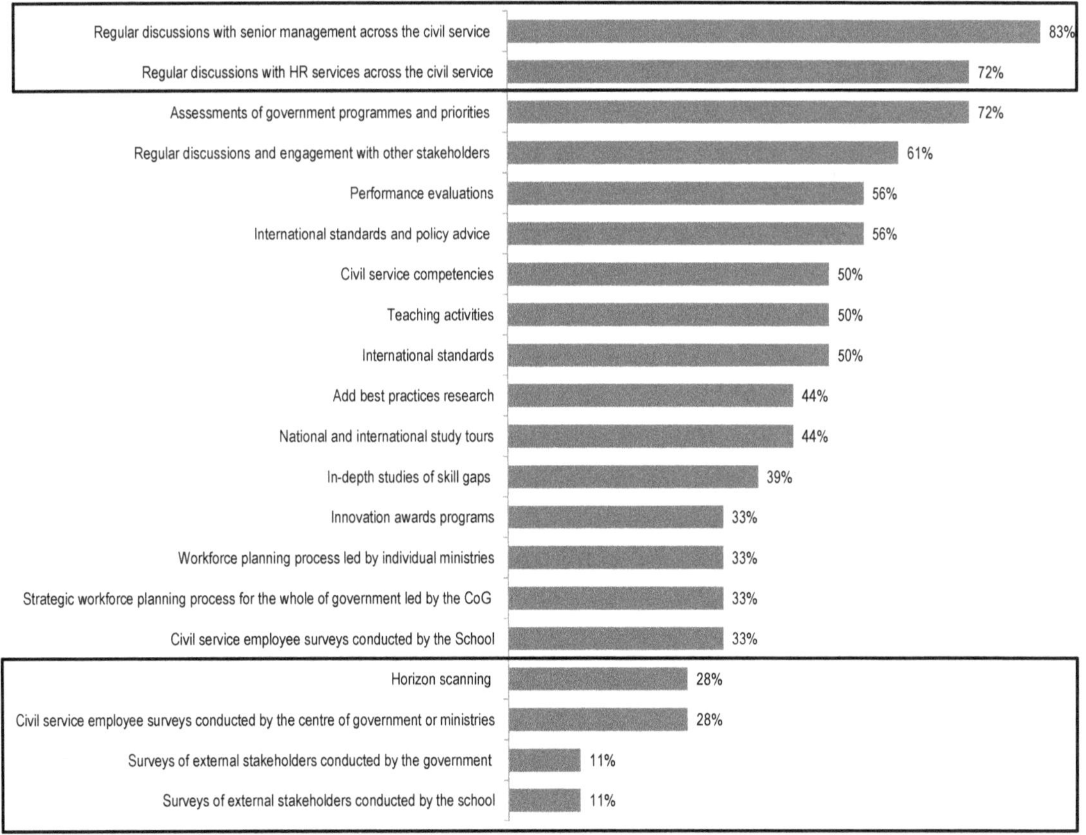

Source: OECD (2014b), "2014 OECD Survey of National Schools of Government".

There are also a number of outward-looking inputs, such as international standards, study tours, or surveys of external stakeholders. While it seems that civil servant knowledge needs are primarily determined based on workplace-defined considerations, some schools of government are able to take into account a broad array of interests.

Alignment with government priorities

Another survey finding concerns the ability of the schools to adapt their learning offerings to the priorities of government. In this area there appears to be a synergy between government priorities and the learning opportunities offered. The existence of this synergy is shown in Figure 2.14, which illustrates the various means that national schools of government use to align their learning offerings with government priorities. For ten schools of government that have responded to the OECD Survey, this entails specifically tailoring learning schemes.

Figure 2.14. **Mechanisms to align government-wide priorities to civil service learning in national schools of government**

Q. What mechanisms are in place for ensuring an alignment between government-wide priorities and learning opportunities available to current and/or future civil servants?

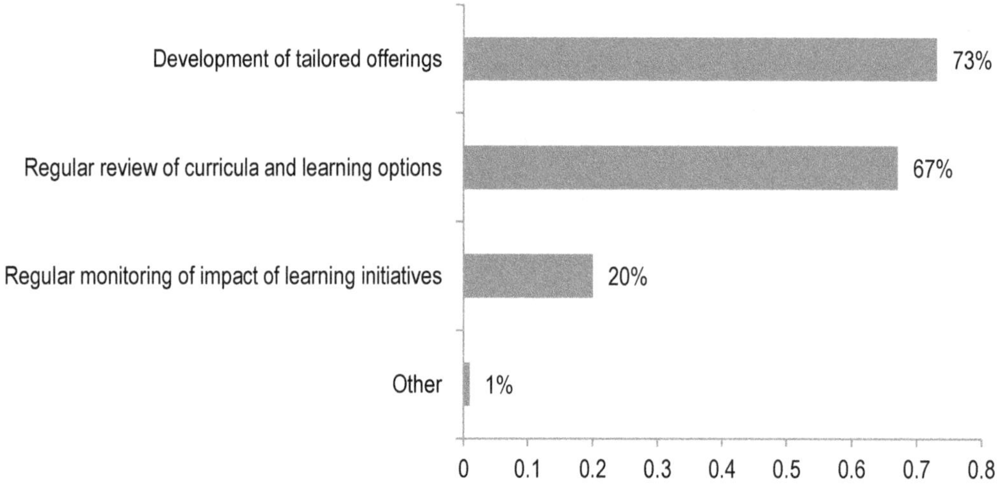

Source: OECD (2014b), "2014 OECD Survey of National Schools of Government".

The OECD Survey also shows that ten schools of government that have responded to the OECD Survey ensure the continued relevance of their civil service learning programmes by providing for the regular review of their curricula. This indicates a high level of awareness of the changing needs of civil servants, and a commitment to keep training programmes relevant and in line with these needs. Beyond highlighting the importance that schools of government give to ensuring that their offerings remain relevant to the current situation faced by governments, this demonstrates there is a clear link between the review of the curricula and the development of tailored course offerings, as the former would naturally be used to identify programme gaps that could be addressed through new offerings. In short, this alignment provides a means to ensure that civil service staff receive training that is not only relevant to their position, but, more importantly, to the context in which they will be fulfilling their duties.

As can be seen in Figure 2.15, most countries use a variety of alignment mechanisms to seek input into the determination of civil service learning priorities. Ten of the responding countries receive their inputs from all four proposed means, with memoranda of understanding (MOU) being the most frequently used. However, across most respondent countries, the relative informality of regular discussions is the most common approach.

There is, in all likelihood, a co-dependence between these alignment mechanisms and their contribution to the development of national civil service learning strategies. This means that discussions concerning learning needs or strategy need to occur before the formalisation of any agreement through an MOU. This also presents the possibility of opening up the process of learning priority identification to several other inputs of information, such as government priorities or employee performance data. In short, the findings of the OECD Survey suggest that, in most countries, this process is fairly broad.

Figure 2.15. **Co-ordination mechanisms to seek input into the determination of civil service learning priorities in national schools of government**

Q. Please describe any co-ordination mechanisms between various levels of government with respect to learning/capability building of future or current civil servants

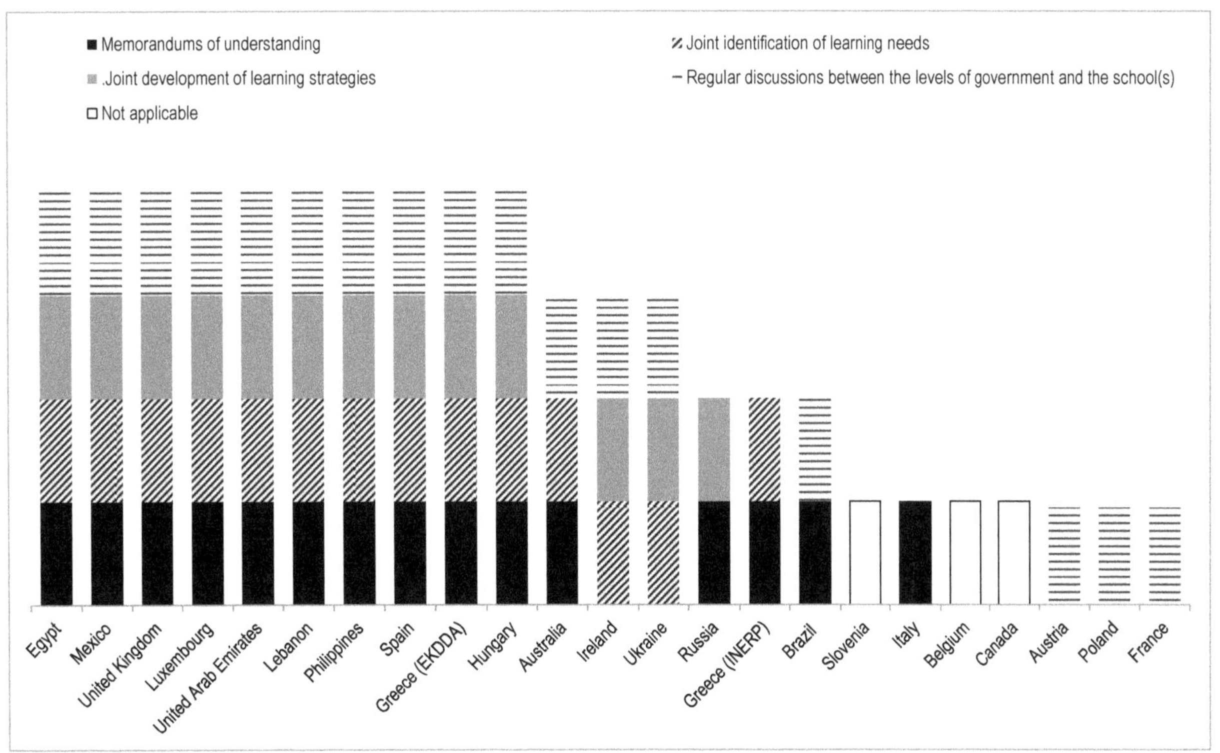

Source: OECD (2014b), "2014 OECD Survey of National Schools of Government".

Actors in aligning learning programmes with government priorities

The OECD Survey also provides information on the actors that are involved in the definition of the civil servant training and professional development priorities. This is another means of exploring a different facet of the link between government priorities, and the development of training and professional development needs. As presented in Figure 2.16, centre of government institutions were identified by schools of government as the single-most influential bodies in the definition of civil service learning priorities in 93% of cases (14 out of 24 respondents) (including Lebanon, Poland and Spain). In another 67% of cases (11 out of 24 respondents), including for Brazil, Luxembourg and the United Arab Emirates, the management of the schools played a key role in defining these priorities. Other governmental institutions, such as ministries, played a role in the process for 60% of respondents (9 out 24 respondents), for example in the Russian Federation.

Figure 2.16. **Actors in priority setting for civil service learning in national schools of government**

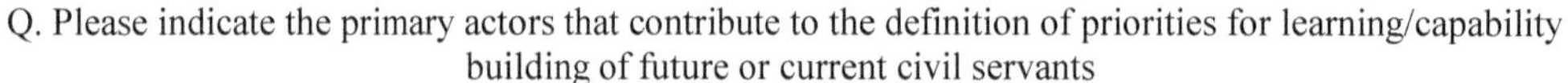

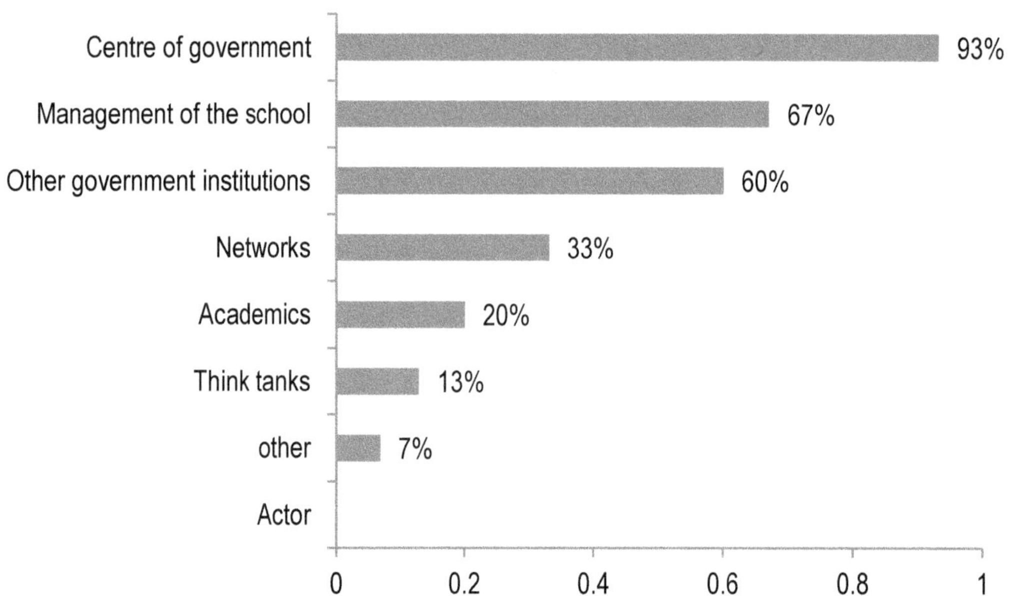

Source: OECD (2014b), "2014 OECD Survey of National Schools of Government".

This finding is consistent with that reported in Figure 2.12, which showed that the principal channel by which the priorities of government are communicated to schools occurs through direct bilateral discussions and meetings with the CoG and other line ministries. This suggests that schools are seeking to acquire information about the priorities of government at the whole-of-government strategic level, although the engagement of external networks and other stakeholders is rarer.

Adjusting to the changing nature of learning needs requires regular adjustment of curricula and various learning programmes. The ability of schools of government to engage COG institutions in this process is critical to ensure that the programmes they offer are aligned with the direction taken by government as a whole. This may be achieved by linking the identification of priorities as a key source in the development of the government-wide and individual ministry learning plans. At the same time, there is also scope for CoG institutions and other institutions of government to proactively engage with schools in order to define the learning needs of civil servants. As noted elsewhere, schools can also play an important role as a source of information for CoG and other civil service institutions through their research activities. In these terms, research contributes to both the development of learning and as an input to government policy and programme development.

Most often schools of government report using the insights gained on the priorities of government to tailor their programme offerings to ensure that these continue to be relevant to the needs and priorities of government. It would however be important to ensure that this is done on a regular basis for the full offerings of schools' programmes, including curricular and learning options, taking into account both the user perspective and broader learning needs.

These findings show that schools of government usually aim to align their programme offerings with both civil service staff and to the broader governmental setting. This requires the regular adjustment of curricula to keep the skills and knowledge of the civil service aligned with the direction taken by government as a whole, as well as adaptable to address complex policy priorities and increasing citizen expectations. This calls for both engagement with central governmental institutions and a broader range of actors outside of government.

Schools of governments' inputs into government priorities

Another consideration is the extent to which schools have the capacity and the opportunity to provide input into the process of priority setting by the government. As institutions often engaged in identifying learning needs and research, schools may be uniquely placed to contribute to the government-wide priorities. Furthermore, by their nature as government-wide service-providing bodies, schools can facilitate linkages between government organisations, thereby encouraging joined-up government.

Irrespective of the institutional relationships that exist between schools and government institutions, schools can serve in both a capacity-building role and as agents of change. In doing so, they can bring to the civil service the ability to learn and promote new ideas and innovations consistent with its mission. However, the ability of schools to undertake these roles depends in large part on their ability to integrate and translate the priorities of the national government into its programming. This highlights a two-way relationship between schools and other institutions of government, also in exchanging information about needs and priorities. It also reflects the importance that the national government places on civil service training and professional development.

Another indicator of the contribution made by schools to the whole of government concerns their participation in the development of government-wide priorities or initiatives, or both. As institutions primarily focused on learning, the schools tend to have less involvement in policy dialogue that define the governmental agenda.

As can be seen in Table 2.1, the involvement of schools of government in the development of government priorities varies considerably among respondents. Although in most cases the schools participated in the definition of the government programme, their contribution was less sustained when other areas of participation are considered. Based on the OECD Survey responses, the schools in Lebanon, Luxembourg, and Ukraine appear the most engaged in governmental priority setting, though only in the four areas most linked to definition of governmental priorities (i.e. government programme, national action plan, national development plan, and other government priority setting).

Table 2.1. **Schools of government contributions to the development of government priorities**

Does the school participate in the development of the following:

	Government programme	National action plan	National development plan	Other government priority setting	Government good practices	Private sector good practices	Non-profit good practices
Belgium	●	❍	❍	❍	❍	❍	❍
Brazil	❍	❍	●	●	❍	❍	❍
Canada	●	❍	❍	●	●	❍	❍
Lebanon	❍	●	●	●	●	❍	❍
Luxembourg	●	●	●	❍	●	❍	❍
Mexico	❍	❍	❍	●	●	❍	❍
Poland	●	❍	❍	❍	●	❍	❍
Russia	●	❍	❍	❍	❍	❍	❍
Slovenia	●	❍	❍	❍	❍	❍	❍
Spain	❍	❍	●	❍	●	❍	❍
Ukraine	●	●	●	❍	●	❍	❍
United Arab Emirates	●	❍	❍	●	●	●	●
●	Yes						
❍	No						

Source: OECD (2014b), "2014 OECD Survey of National Schools of Government".

Although less relevant to the development of government priorities, it is noteworthy that the vast majority of schools were also involved in the development of government good practice (8 out of 12 respondents), perhaps stemming directly from their mandate as training institutions.

As shown in Table 2.2, for the schools that do participate in the definition of the governmental agenda, they do so mainly through the ranges of events and conferences (as highlighted by all respondents) rather than undertaking research and generating evidence to promote policy dialogue (3 out of 11 respondents to this question in both cases). This suggests that the contribution of schools to priority setting is primarily as a convenor of government-wide dialogue. Among the respondents, only the United Arab Emirates' Mohammed Bin Rashid School reported contributing via all three means, which may be explained by the unique nature of the institution and its close ties to government, as discussed later.

Table 2.2. **Schools of government contributions to whole-of-government initiatives**

Q. Basis of participation in whole-of-government in the development of government priorities, as follows:

	Robust research programme	Events and conferences	Generation of evidence and data to support policy dialogue	Other
Belgium	❍	●	❍	❍
Brazil	❍	●	❍	●
Canada	❍	●	❍	●
Lebanon	❍	●	●	❍
Luxembourg	❍	●	❍	❍
Mexico	❍	●	❍	●
Russia	❍	●	●	❍
Slovenia	❍	●	❍	❍
Spain	●	●	❍	❍
Ukraine	●	●	❍	❍
United Arab Emirates	●	●	●	❍
●	Yes			
❍	No			

Source: OECD (2014b), "2014 OECD Survey of National Schools of Government".

Overall, schools tend to engage in the process of informing national priorities, though this engagement primarily derives from their convening power rather than direct influence. The factors underlying this may derive from the schools' institutional features, the nature of their linkages with the CoG, and the activities in which they engage, for example in the area of research.

Assessment and recommendations

Schools of government have a strategic potential to contribute to the effectiveness and efficiency of government, by supporting the development of skills and competencies in civil services. As governments grapple with strained budgets, training and development becomes a strategic choice for governments seeking to contend with emerging technological and managerial changes. This includes the need to develop skills and capacity for better management and delivery of public services in an era of changing citizen expectations and new policy challenges.

As discussed, though most governments have identified the key civil service competencies and skills, with the exception of values, these tend to be mainly defined for specific job categories. Though determining competencies and skills for an entire civil service may prove a complex task, there is perhaps greater scope to do so for certain core competencies. Because of their whole-of-government mandate, most schools are also well positioned to identify the skills and behaviours required by all employees, irrespective of their job or function.

In addition, given the link between training, development and competency development, it seems important to involve schools of government in the process of competency identification and monitoring. Building on good practices identified by many participating schools of government, it is also important to ensure that these linkages are captured in a government-wide strategy for civil service learning, which could be linked to civil service competencies.

The organisation of civil service learning and development varies greatly by country, reflecting differing policy choices and the institutional make-up of the national government. As a result, in several countries the responsibility for a learning and development strategy falls to the ministry or department rather than at a whole-of-government level. In such cases, schools can play an important role in ensuring that these organisational learning strategies are aligned and co-ordinated with the whole-of-government objectives.

At the same time, it is important to ensure that the various strands of civil service human resources management are linked together in the organisation and delivery of learning and development programmes, such as employee learning and performance management. This is needed to ensure that employees receive the training they need to continue to perform their duties as well as to enhance the effectiveness of governments thanks to well-trained and high-performing employees.

Ensuring that civil service capacity keeps up with new and evolving government missions in light of changing circumstances and evolving citizen expectations is paramount. Looking forward, it will be important to ensure that schools preserve the ability to intervene in the development of civil service capacity. This will require the review and revision, as necessary, of the legal instruments or policies that define the mandate and mission of the schools. These reviews will ensure that schools can address the challenges and needs of civil services in the present and near future.

A similar issue concerns the identification of skills gaps across civil service. schools of government are well placed to participate in the identification of the needed skills given that many of them have a whole-of-government mandate. For the most part, the findings of the OECD Survey confirm that schools of government are indeed involved in this process. However, this occurs as part of a process that involves few external parties as such, possibly limiting the ability to take into account emerging factors and trends that may in time affect governments. In order to identify skills gaps in a more holistic way, more systematic approaches to public consultation and trend identification are needed.

While schools are increasingly expected to align their learning and development programmes with government priorities to ensure that civil servants have the knowledge, competencies and skills to deal with current and emerging policy priorities, for the most part the identification of government priorities appears to be achieved through formal and unstructured means – principally through meetings and bilateral exchanges. While these are useful means to gain insights into governmental directions, an approach based on a larger number of inputs may prove more informative and inclusive. At the same time, governments may also benefit from establishing more robust channels to obtain insight from schools of government, especially those that engage in research and knowledge development. In short, a reciprocal exchange between schools of government and other government institutions, particularly centre of government institutions, may contribute to strengthening the linkage between government priorities and learning.

In light of the above, schools of government may consider the following recommendations:

- **Recommendation 2.1**: Develop channels to effectively contribute to defining the core competencies required across civil services.
- **Recommendation 2.2**: Support the design and implementation of whole-of-government and organisation-specific civil service learning and development strategies. Where these strategies apply to national and sub-national governments,

work with all actors to ensure that the alignment of the learning strategy to the development and delivery of civil service learning programmes.

- **Recommendation 2.3**: Promote the development and use of employee learning plans that take into consideration employee performance and organisational needs.
- **Recommendation 2.4**: Regularly consult with internal and external stakeholders on the identification of civil service skills gaps and learning priorities as part of the process of developing learning programmes.
- **Recommendation 2.5**: Develop the systematic and comprehensive approaches to identify current and emerging government priorities and external trends in order to inform the development of civil service learning and development programmes.
- **Recommendation 2.6**: Regularly review schools' learning and development programmes to ensure that these take into account current and potential future needs and priorities of governments and civil servants.

Notes

1. The OECD has also developed the concept of competencies as part of its Skills Beyond Schools initiative (OECD, 2014a).
2. See, for example, National Audit Office, 2011.
3. See also Australian Public Service Commission and Australian National Audit Office, 2003.
4. Examples of such professions include physicians, lawyers and engineers.

References

Australian Public Service Commission and Australian National Audit Office (2003), "Building Capability: A Framework for Managing Learning and Development in the APS", Australian Public Service Commission.

Civil Service Human Resources (2015), "Civil Service Competency Framework 2012-2017", Civil Service Human Resources, London, United Kingdom, www.gov.uk/government/uploads/system/uploads/attachment_data/file/436073/cscf_fulla4potrait_2013-2017_v2d.pdf.

Civil Service Training and Development (2011), "Learning and Development Framework for the Civil Service, 2011-2014", Civil Service Training and Development, Ireland, http://hr.per.gov.ie/wp-content/uploads/2011/04/Learning-and-Development-Framework.pdf.

Deloitte (2015), *Global Human Capital Trends 2015: Leading in the New World of Work*, Deloitte University Press.

Dickinson, H. (2013), "The 21st century public servant", *The Guardian*, 30 April, www.theguardian.com/society/2013/apr/30/21st-century-public-service-skills.

Dickinson, H. and H. Sullivan (2014), *Imagining the 21st Century Public Service Workforce,* University of Melbourne, Melbourne, http://bespoke-production.s3.amazonaws.com/msog/assets/b7/d2ec80db6d11e58244af312943873d/MSoG-21c-Draft2_2_.pdf.

Dobos, A. (2015), "Professional development in the civil service - From American and Hungarian perpectives", *Procedia - Social and Behaviourial Sciences*, 191, pp. 1886-18890, http://dx.doi.org/10.1016/j.sbspro.2015.04.706.

Government of British Columbia (n.d.), "Development the Best: A Corporate Learning Strategy for the BC Public Service", Public Service Agency, Victoria, British Columbia, www2.gov.bc.ca/local/myhr/documents/learning_education/corporate_learning_strategy.pdf.

International Labour Office (2010), *A Skilled Workforce for Strong, Sustainable and Balanced Growth: A G20 Training Strategy*, International Labour Office, Geneva.

Medland, D. (2013), "Working in the public sector: Enterpreneurial skills top the wanted list", *The Financial Times*, 17 March, www.ft.com/cms/s/0/af6f5f9e-9186-11e2-b839-00144feabdc0.html#axzz3nhlqiPVv.

National Audit Office (2011), "Identifying and meeting Central Government's skills requirements", National Audit Office, London, United Kingdom.

Needham, C. and C. Mangan (2015), *The 21st Century Public Servant*, Public Sector Academy, University of Birmingham, Birmingham, http://pure-oai.bham.ac.uk/ws/files/27714134/The_21st_century_public_servant_working_at_three_boundaries_of_public_and_private.pdf.

OECD (forthcoming), "National Schools of Government Network Annual Meeting 2016: Summary report", OECD.

OECD (2015a), *Government at a Glance 2015*, OECD Publishing, Paris, http://dx.doi.org/10.1787/gov_glance-2015-en.

OECD (2015b), *Building on Basics*, OECD Publishing, Paris, http://dx.doi.org/10.1787/9789264235052-en.

OECD (2014a), *Skills beyond School: Synthesis Report*, OECD Publishing, Paris, http://dx.doi.org/10.1787/9789264214682-en.

OECD (2014b), "2014 OECD Survey of National Schools of Government".

OECD (2011), *Public Servants as Partners for Growth: Toward a Stronger, Leaner and More Equitable Workforce*, OECD Publishing, Paris, http://dx.doi.org/10.1787/9789264166707-en.

Rajasekar, J. and S. A. Khan (2013), "Training and development function in Omani public sector organizations", *Journal of Applied Business and Economics*, 14(2), pp. 37-52.

Reichard, C. (1998), "Education and training for new public management", *International Public Management Journal,* 1(2), pp. 177-194.

ReSPA (Regional School of Public Administration) (2008), *Civil Service Training Systems in the Western Balkans Region*, ReSPA, Montenegro.

Treasury Board Secretariat (2016), "Key Leadership Competency profile and examples of effective and ineffective behaviours", Treasury Board Secretariat, Government of Canada, www.tbs-sct.gc.ca/psm-fpfm/learning-apprentissage/pdps-ppfp/klc-ccl/klcp-pccl-eng.asp.

Treasury Board Secretariat (2008), "Policy on Learning, Training and Development", Treasury Board Secretariat, Government of Canada, www.tbs-sct.gc.ca/pol/doc-eng.aspx?id=12405.

United Nations Public Administration Network (n.d.), "Rethinking public administration: An overview", United Nations Public Administraton Network, New York, www.unpan.org/Portals/0/60yrhistory/documents/Publications/Rethinking%20public%20administration.pdf.

Chapter 3

Innovating in schools of government programmes

The tools and technologies with which civil servants need to work have become increasingly sophisticated. This chapter considers the teaching and research activities of the schools of government through the lens of innovation and the increasing need for schools to keep pace with evolving technologies. The chapter provides an overview of the modern means and innovations used by schools of government to deliver training, learning and professional development opportunities to public servants.

Introduction

While schools of government (or "schools") generally serve as institutions focused on the learning and development needs of civil service employees, there is a wide range of organisational forms, structures, mandates, and approaches to, and nature of, training and development. While some operate in ways similar to institutions like colleges or universities, others focus primarily on development of senior civil servants. As such, the nature of their training and development activities vary considerably. Some of these differences are explored below.

In view of growing competition from other training providers, increasingly scarce resources, varying types of learning needs and changing citizen expectations, schools are increasingly looking to new and innovative approaches to deliver learning, including the integration of information and communication technologies (ICTs). At the same time, the pace, types and approaches to adopting innovative training and development techniques vary significantly across schools, which may also reflect the challenges in developing and implementing innovative methods that continue to generate appropriate learning outcomes and client satisfaction. The impacts on learning outcomes as well as on the increased ability of schools to respond to government priorities are still to be assessed. In this context, this chapter provides an overview of the means and recent innovations used by schools of government to deliver training, learning and professional development opportunities to public servants.

Civil service learning and development approaches

The approaches to learning and development used by schools of government are often strongly dependent on the type of their mandates. Those schools mandated to deliver post-secondary education are more likely to be highly invested in teaching and research. This will typically entail providing longer programmes, e.g. graduate programmes requiring 200 hours of study or diploma programmes requiring 100 hours. As a result, these programmes may involve a higher percentage of time spent in classroom-based learning, such as seminars and lectures, and involve evaluation of student assessments to enable credentials to be conferred. By contrast, schools with a mandate to provide professional development and training to current public servants tend to focus on shorter term activities, such as two- and three-day training programmes, and are more likely to adopt experimental learning approaches. These programmes typically do not involve student assessments and increasingly rely on alternatives to classroom-based learning. This being said, there are a significant number of schools of government that provide both types of learning activities, resulting in blending employment and learning models (OECD, forthcoming).

The integration of governmental priorities into learning and development activities of schools may take several forms (see Chapter 2). As revealed by the 2014 OECD Survey of National Schools of Government (or "OECD Survey"), schools tend to use a wide array of sources of information to inform the process of developing skills-based learning and professional development programmes, including evaluation results, performance management results, policy scans, and research findings.

One way to consider the effectiveness of schools of government programmes is to analyse the extent to which the existing demand for specific skills and competencies from civil service is met by the offerings of learning and development programmes, both in terms of the programme delivery methods and content. When considering the top most ranked learning areas offered by schools and the potential skills needs in civil services, there seems to be relative alignment between the two (see Table 3.1). Although some disparities exist, people management, ICT applications, change management and project management are the areas highly ranked as both learning offerings and skills needs. Looking at the themes individually, organisational effectiveness and people management are the primary themes identified both for training and skills development. Other priority training and development areas are budgeting and financial management, civil service values and ethics, and change management; these do not fully align with priority areas for skills development, although they are, nonetheless, important for a well-performing civil service.

Table 3.1. **Main areas of learning and development offered by schools of government and civil service skills gaps**

Q. Please provide information on the governance areas in which your school provides learning and developmental opportunities and accompanying methods for building capabilities. Please also indicate if any of the below skills are lacking in the civil service.

Most provided learning and development opportunities	Civil service skills gaps
1. People management	1. Change management
2. Budgeting and financial management	2. Risk evaluation
3. Information management and new technology applications	3. Information management and new technology applications
4. Openness, transparency, and accountability	4. People management
5. Management of networks and partnerships	5. Project management
6. Organisational effectiveness	6. Regulatory management
7. Civil service values and ethics	7. Relationships with external stakeholders
8. Change management	8. Policy and programme evaluation
9. Project management	9. Innovation
10. Organisational behaviour	10. Policy and programme formulation and analysis

Source: OECD (2014), "2014 OECD Survey of National Schools of Government".

At the same time, while risk evaluation, programme evaluation, innovation, stakeholder engagement and policy analysis have been identified among the areas with greatest skills gaps across civil services, learning offerings in these areas generally appear to be scarce. This may prove detrimental to the capacity of the civil service to respond to emerging needs. Some of the reasons for these gaps may derive from the time lag in development of new learning and training offerings, institutional path dependency and limited financial resources.

Specific national circumstances may also influence the nature of learning and development programmes. For example, some European respondents noted that the required training for their staff included matters relevant to the country's membership in the European Union (e.g. Spain), while others identified training of a more generalised nature (e.g. Poland).

Finally, with regard to leadership development, a number of schools providing such services underlined the importance of utilising a combination of training and development methods (coaching, classroom training, feedback and experiential training), including methods that can improve leaders' knowledge and self-awareness. In this context, schools of government with the mandate to support leadership development are faced with pressure to demonstrate their capacity to provide high-quality activities, also in view of strong competition from external training providers.

Models of civil service training, learning and professional development programmes

There is considerable literature on the lifelong acquisition of skills and knowledge and how to provide continuing education to professionals. It underlines the importance of understanding the relationship between learning and employment and the need for ongoing adaptation of approaches to training and development to respond to client needs. Beyond traditional training, there appears to be a common acceptance that the best context for learning is through practice and learning from peers as a means of drawing on shared experience and expertise. In addition, learning centred on problem-solving has also shown itself to be an effective way to structure professional learning (Boud and Hager, 2011).

Though there are multiple approaches to providing training to civil services, 93% of respondents to the OECD Survey (14 out of 15 institutions) indicated a preference for traditional classroom training. Other teaching methods, such as team-based activities and study tours are also being used, though by less than 50% of schools. However, there is a growing movement towards the convergence of various means of training delivery, as each method provides unique advantages that may prove complementary. For example, in-service and executive training use a variety of delivery methods as part of their programmes and also integrate a degree of peer-learning and problem-solving approaches as they tend to be backed up by in-service training. This combination allows for skills taught in seminars and workshops to be subsequently reinforced with more practical applications within the work environment. This is considered a strong teaching method, as it allows individuals in training to better assimilate and internalise the skills they are taught (Goldsmith and Carter, 2009).

In addition, traditional learning approaches may prove less applicable to an operating context defined by extensive budget cutbacks, restructured programmes and an ever-increasing need to justify public expenditures on training. In this context, classroom training is resource intensive and limited in its reach. Another emerging factor is the entry of a new generation of employees into the civil service, many of them having grown up with information technology, and for whom online courses, wikis, and social networks are the preferred means of learning.

As a result, though classroom learning remains by far the primary means of learning, schools are increasing their online learning offers. While still a minority, four schools that have responded to the OECD Survey are providing training to civil servants in the form of online self-study courses. For example, Canada's Canada School of Public Service (CSPS) offers nearly 100 courses that are available for online self-study in a variety of administrative and policy areas, such as values and ethics, language training, and risk management, to name a few (CSPS, 2015). In other case, one school is using information technology as a tool to increase the reach of their course offerings.

This comparatively low-rate of adoption of digital technologies for learning may partly stem from the lack of existing policies or guidelines to guide their use. Only half of survey respondents reported having an explicit policy for the use of digital technologies for the learning of current and future public servants in place (see Victoria State Government, 2015 and National Education Association, 2015 as examples of available guidelines). Effective implementation of e-learning and other innovative training methods may also require significant initial investments and a civil service culture tolerant of risk-taking and potential failures, as the outcomes of innovative approaches are often difficult to predict. Robust evaluation approaches to learning and development innovations, as well as pilot initiatives, can help minimise the risk of large-scale failures and roll out the initiatives on a wider scale.

Looking to the future, schools may consider developing more proactive approaches and greater investments into innovative training and learning methods, in view of budget restraint, strong competition, the changing nature of learners and learning, and the increased preponderance of e-learning technologies. Offering combined delivery methods may satisfy the diverse needs of learners and enable schools to achieve cost savings. Investment in the development of currently lacking priority skills for public servants, such as risk management and policy analysis, will also be critical to ensure the ongoing relevance of schools' programmes.

Training allowances

National civil service learning strategies and plans, as well as negotiated collective agreements, provide the framework for civil servant access to learning and development opportunities. As the OECD first observed in 1997 (OECD, 1997), the ability of civil servants to obtain training should be considered as an integral part of their duties. This principle is captured in the United Kingdom's Civil Service Capability Plan (UK Government, 2014), which outlines the training entitlement for members of the civil service.

Across OECD countries, the average number of training days allocated to civil service employees varies greatly by country. For example, the average length of training received by employees ranges from low of one to three days annually in Germany to high of seven to ten days annually in Italy (OECD, 2010). The findings of the OECD Survey are broadly aligned with these figures, as the majority of respondents reported the average length of civil service training as less than five days. However, the OECD Survey also suggests that the length of training varied across employment categories. Whereas current and entry-level civil servants received training of less than five days in duration, a significant percentage of respondents noted that middle and senior managers received training of more than five days.

Induction programmes for new staff have increasingly been recognised as beneficial to staff effectiveness as they promote understanding about roles and responsibilities (CIPD, 2016). In some OECD countries training is considered a key part of the induction process for new civil servants and is mandatory. In addition, 85% of OECD Survey respondents cited the requirement for civil servants in their countries to receive annual training as an integral part of their duties. Similarly, the OECD Survey found that in 60% of cases a training requirement for middle and senior management ranks was also mandatory, and in about half of these cases the training was mandatory for all new recruits upon entry to the civil service. These figures are comparable to results from a previous OECD study (OECD, 2013, p. 87).

However, no clear pattern emerged with regard to the topics covered by the mandatory training, although civil service values, core competencies, occupational skills and management skills were all equally represented. This can be partially explained by the broad array of civil service roles, which makes the development of training that is relevant to all civil service staff a complex task. Thus, outside of topics such as civil service values, which are equally relevant to all staff, mandatory training focused on particularly functional needs may be the preferable approach.

The OECD Survey also found that formalised training to enter the civil service is not uniformly required across the respondent countries. Countries that do require entry training (Belgium, Canada, Luxembourg and the United Kingdom), tend to feature a career-based civil service. The United Kingdom features a position-based civil service system with career elements. Australia requires from staff new to the Australian Public Service (APS) to complete the APS induction programme that ensure that candidates are aware of their obligations and able to meet the expectations placed on them (see Box 3.1).

Box 3.1. **Australia Public Service induction programme**

The programme consists of ten modules covering core knowledge that is essential for working in the Australia Public Service (APS). Key topics include: the structure of government; the APS ethical and legal framework; governance; and workforce diversity. These modules each take between 15-30 minutes to complete. Although there is a progressive flow between the modules, there is flexibility to undertake them in any order or discreetly.

While it is expected that the online programme will be an easily accessible, flexible component of agency induction and graduate programmes, it will also be an essential means for experienced APS staff to update themselves on the recent changes to the Public Service Act 1999, especially in the areas of values, ethics, code of conduct and the new employment principles.

Source: Australian Government (2013), "Australian Public Service induction", Australian Public Service Commission, www.apsc.gov.au/working-in-the-aps/apsinduction.

Programme accreditation and standards of excellence

With the rapid internationalisation of higher education and the expansion of cross-border student, programme and institutional mobility, quality assurance is increasingly the focus of national governments and the schools. These developments are accompanied by increasing awareness of the strong links between quality assurance, qualifications recognition and international quality labelling through evaluation and accreditation processes (Box 3.2). The accreditation, irrespective of whether it is done by a national regulator or an international organisation, is seen as an important ingredient for improvement of programmes and teaching quality. It can also result in convergence and a common interdisciplinary perception of public administration programmes between and within schools and lead to adjustments in the programme structure, critical review of the content of the curricula, teaching methods and facilities, which can ultimately support the increased quality of the programme (Reichard, 2010). It can also involve a reflection of qualifications and sufficiency of staff to train the students adequately, feasibility of the programme and the approaches to evaluations of acquired skills and development Yet, practitioners note a number of challenges related to accreditation (de Vries, 2014). First is the differences in the framing of the public administration discipline across the countries (as in some countries public administration originates from faculties of law, in others – of political science or business administration and economics. According to Hajnal (2003), public administration programmes could be divided into a business group (e.g. Denmark,

Norway, Latvia, the Czech Republic and Slovakia), a policy / administration group (e.g. Germany, France) and a legal group (e.g. Poland, Hungary, Portugal, Italy and Greece). Another related challenge, according de Vries, is the agreement on what constitutes "a good study" in public administration – if it is a study about or for administration, which in turn imply different teaching approaches and thematic focus.

Box 3.2. Programme accreditation approaches

Some of the main organisations involved in learning programme accreditation include EAPAA (The European Association for Public Administration Accreditation), NASPAA (the accreditation organization for PA programs in the USA) and CIAPA (the recently established accreditation organization for accreditation of public administration programs within the International Association of Schools and Institutes in Administration).

The process of accreditation is mostly standardized: the board of the accreditation organization in question makes a decision to accredit or not to accredit a program in public administration that has requested such accreditation. The request is based on a report from a site-visit team of international experts in public administration and peers that has examined the quality of the program during a short visit to the university and its judgment of a previously written self-evaluation provided by the institute requesting accreditation.

NASPAA's accreditation process, driven by public service values, is mission- and outcomes-based, and grounded in an in-depth self-evaluation of programs using the NASPAA Accreditation Standards. Programs seeking accreditation use the self-study process to support ongoing program improvement, strengthen their commitment to public service education, and showcase their accomplishments. Accredited programs must contribute to the knowledge, research, and practice of public service, establish observable goals and outcomes, and use information about their performance to guide program improvement.

EAPAA is Europe's accreditation agency in public administration education as proofed by the European Quality Assurance Registry for Higher Education (EQAR). EAPAA has been reviewed and accepted by the International Network for Quality Assurance Agencies in Higher Education (INQAAHE), a world-wide association of over 200 organisations active in the theory and practice of quality assurance in higher education. It focuses on public administration, public policy and public management programmes.

CIPA (the International Commission on Accreditation of Public Administration Education and Training Programmes) has been appointed in August 2012. It is responsible for developing and initiating a process for the accreditation of public administration education and training programs, building on the joint United Nations/IASIA report on Standards of Excellence for Public Administration Education and Training.

Source: de Vries, M. (2014), "International Accreditation of PA Programs: Narrations of an Evaluator, *The NISPAcee Journal of Public Administration and Policy*, Vol. VI, No. 2, www.degruyter.com/downloadpdf/j/nispa.2013.6.issue-2/nispa-2013-0008/nispa-2013-0008.pdf.

In parallel with the accreditation efforts, the Division of Public Administration and Development Management of the United Nations Department of Economic and Social Affairs (UN/DPADM) and the International Association of Schools and Institutes of Administration (IASIA) have initiated the work on defining the standards of excellence for programmes on public administration and training. The work has resulted in the identification of eight Standards of Excellence (Box 3.3), which included specific for potential assessment of quality of programmes.

Box 3.3. UN/IASIA Standards of Excellence for Public Administration Education and Training

The Task Force of established the following eight Standards of Excellence for Public Administration Education and Training:

1. Public Service Commitment: The faculty and administration of the program are defined by their fundamental commitment to public service. They are, in all of their activities (teaching, training, research, technical assistance and other service activities), at all times absolutely committed to the advancement of the public interest and the building of democratic institutions.
2. Advocacy of Public Interest Values: The program's faculty and administration reflect their commitment to the advancement of public service by both their advocacy for, and their efforts to create, a culture of participation, commitment, responsiveness and accountability in all of those organizations and institutions with which they come into contact.
3. Combining Scholarship, Practice and Community Service: Because public administration is an applied science, the faculty and administration of the program are committed to the integration of theory and practice and, as such, the program draws upon knowledge and understanding generated both by the highest quality of research and the most outstanding practical experience.
4. The Faculty are Central: The commitment and quality of the faculty (and/or trainers) is central to the achievement of program goals in all areas of activity. Consequently, there must be a full-time, core faculty committed to the highest standards of teaching, training and research and possessing the authority and responsibility appropriate to accepted standards of faculty program governance. This faculty must be paid at a level that allows them to devote the totality of their professional activities to the achievements of the goals and purposes of the program and must be available in adequate numbers consistent with the mission of the program.
5. Inclusiveness is at the Heart of the Programme: A critical element in the achievement of excellence in public administration education and training is an unwavering commitment on the part of faculty and administration to the diversity of ideas and participation. The people who participate in programs, including students, trainees, trainers, administrators and faculty, should come from all of the different racial, ethnic, and demographic communities of the society. The ideas, concepts, theories and practices addressed in the program should represent a broad variety of intellectual interests and approaches.
6. A Curriculum that is Purposeful and Responsive: A principal goal of public administration education and training is the development of public administrators who will make strong, positive contributions to the public service generally and, in particular, to the organizations they join, or to which they return. This requires public administration education and training programs to have coherent missions which drive program organization and curriculum development. In addition, it is critical that those who educate and train public administrators communicate and work with and, as appropriate, be responsive to the organizations for which they are preparing students and trainees.
7. Adequate Resources are Critical: An important prerequisite to creating a program of excellence in public administration education and training is the availability of adequate resources. Many different kinds of resources are required including facilities, technology, library resources and student services (in terms of assistance with meeting such basic needs as housing, health care, etc.). The availability of these resources is a function of the availability of adequate financial resources.
8. Balancing Collaboration and Competition: There must be among the program faculty, trainers, administrators and students and/or trainees a sense of common purpose and mission deriving from the program's commitment to the advancing of the public interest. There must also be a sense of determination, indeed, even competitiveness, that drives the program to be the best and creates a desire to meet and exceed world class standards of excellence.

Source: Rosenbaum, Allan (ed.) (2015), *In Quest of Excellence: Approaches to Enhancing the Quality of Public Administration Education and Training*, NISPAcee, Slovensko.

Knowledge development and research

The OECD Survey reveals that in the context of a knowledge economy, more than half of responding schools of government have a twin mandate to provide both learning programmes and to engage in knowledge development and research. Research is conducted to support both the identification of civil service priorities and to strengthen the evidence base for their programmes. Knowledge development and research often serve as a source of new insights and innovation in terms of knowledge, skills, and learning and development techniques and approaches.

As shown in Figure 3.1, 60 % of OECD Survey respondents (18 out of 23) indicated that they are engaged in knowledge development and research activities, though in just over half of the cases (56% or 13 out of 23 respondents) this consisted primarily of applied research.[1] By contrast, research defined as academic was pursued by just over 10% (3 out of 23 respondents).

Figure 3.1. **Knowledge development and research in national schools of government**

Q. Is the school engaged in knowledge development and research?

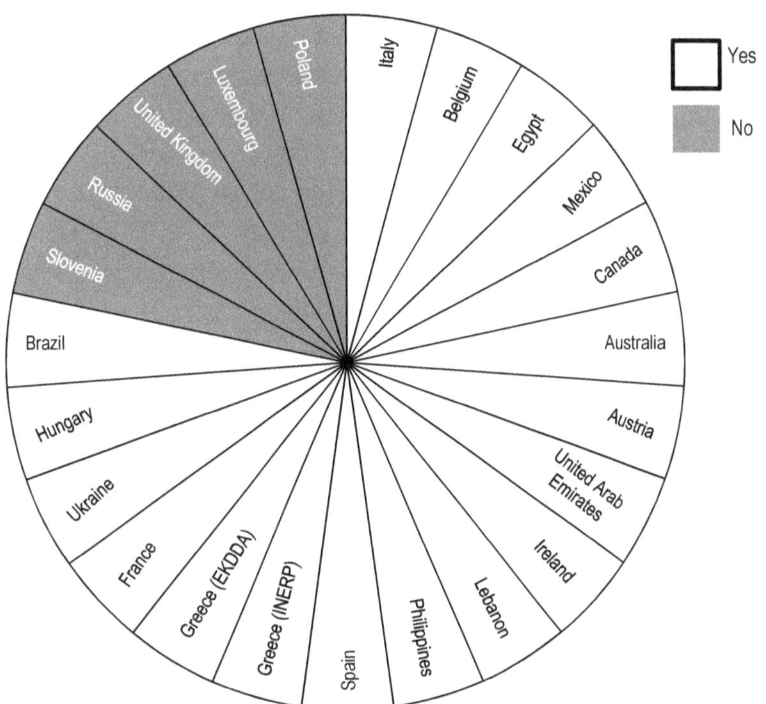

Source: OECD (2014), "2014 OECD Survey of National Schools of Government".

For those schools that reported the existence of a research programme, 89% report that the purpose of this programme was to promote better services and policies, while 78% indicated that it served to deepen the understanding of the functioning of the civil service. Another 67% stated that the purpose of research programmes was to address knowledge gaps to promote the improvement of the civil service. Overall, for the schools with a research programme, such programmes tend to focus mainly on the areas where schools provide training and development programmes (with the exception of information technology, project management and administrative law).

In terms of research priorities, 46% of OECD Survey respondents identified institutional and organisational transformation, with 31% of respondents identifying innovation as a priority research area (see Figure 3.2). Other research priorities reported by the schools include people management and policy and programme evaluation. Moreover, it is likely that several of these research areas are being pursued jointly given their complementarity, such as organisational behaviour, institutional and organisational transformation, and change management.

Figure 3.2. **Research priorities in national schools of government**

Q. Please select top five priority themes for research in your school

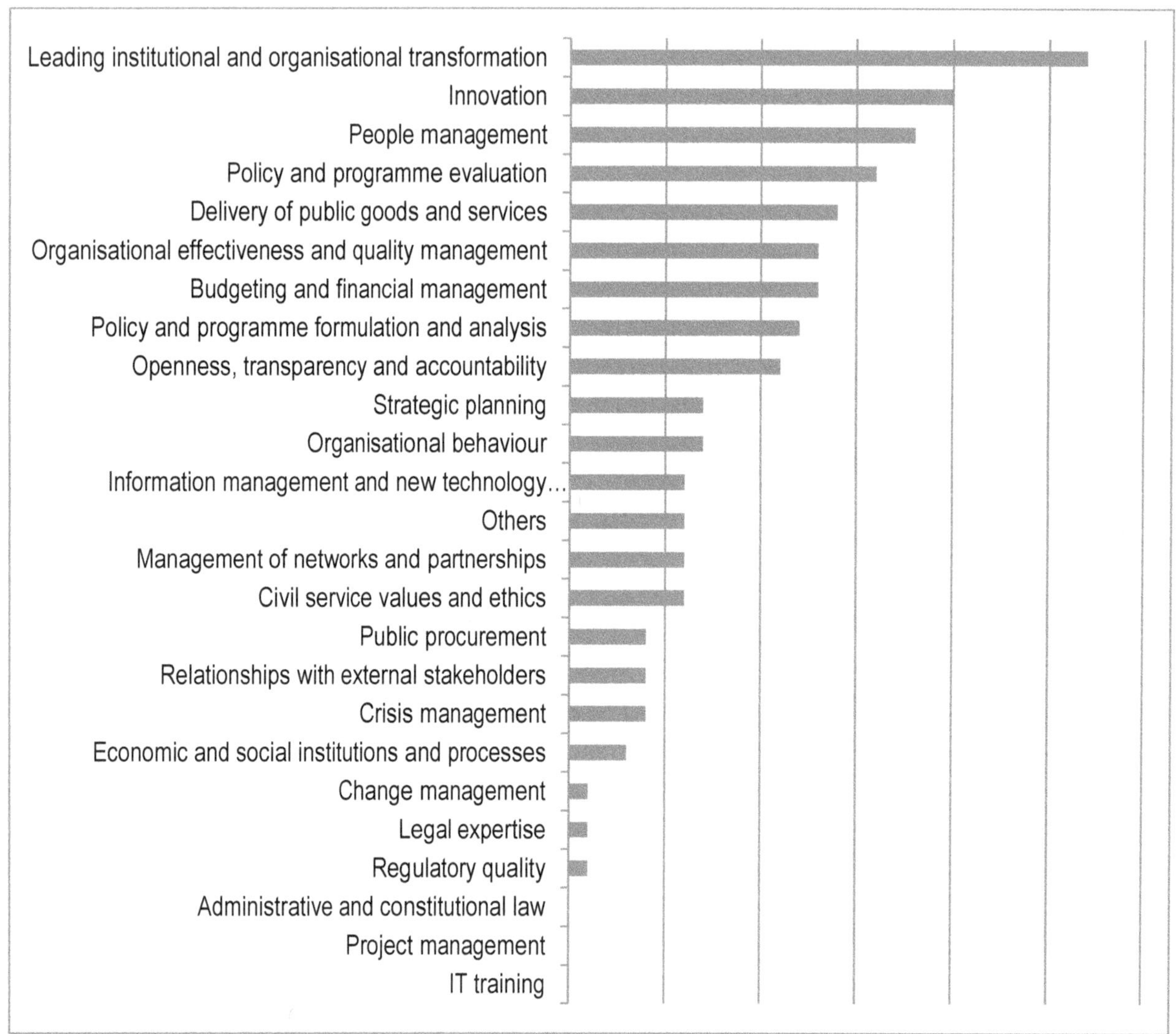

Source: OECD (2014), "2014 OECD Survey of National Schools of Government".

Priority research areas also appear to be aligned with the areas with current skills gaps, as discussed above. In addition, 55% of OEC Survey respondents reported that their research was used as an input into government decision making.

Indeed, as is the case with the definition of the teaching priorities of schools, the process by which research priorities are determined is also open to multiple inputs. The OECD Survey identified two main sources of the definition of schools' research priorities. These include assessments of government programmes and priorities, and regular discussions with senior management across the civil service (see Figure 3.3). To ensure relevance of both research and training and development programmes, it will be important to ensure their ongoing alignment with the government's current and future agendas.

Figure 3.3. **Who contributes to the definition of learning priorities for civil servants in national schools of government**

Q. Please indicate the primary actors that contribute to the definition of priorities for learning/capability building of future or current civil servants

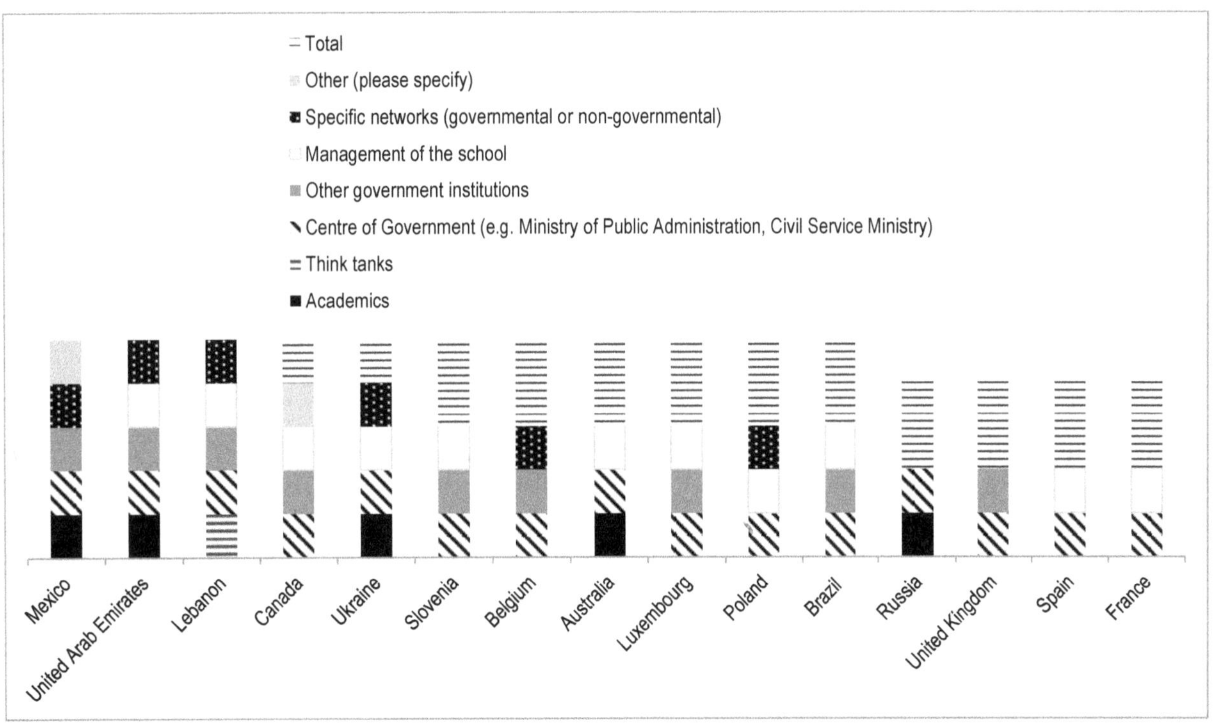

Source: OECD (2014), "2014 OECD Survey of National Schools of Government".

Though not examined by the OECD Survey, it is also likely that the research priorities of individual staff members of schools may be defined by their professional interests – often supported by internal or external research grants – rather than by institutional or government priorities. This may be the case where schools of government are degree-granting higher education institutions. In these cases, the research norms and practices would be closer to those of a university rather than those of a government institution.

Assessment and recommendations

Teaching, and in many cases, research seem to be an integral part of the core mandate of schools of government. Given the unique skills needs for civil services, schools of government can play a central role in providing the necessary training and development opportunities, given their mandates and proximity to the government. This also means that in a context of diminishing resources, schools are making strategic choices about how to invest in the design, development and delivery of courses and programmes where they have a unique value-added for civil services.

At the same time, strong competition from the private sector and other training providers calls on schools to embed innovative learning methods, including through the accreditation processes, that can ensure responsiveness to the needs of individual learners and the government as whole, while achieving cost savings, such as e-learning. Yet the progress appears relatively slow. For example, on e-learning, some of the barriers appear to relate to the lack of policies and guidelines on the use of information and communication technologies and social media in the civil service.

In addition, ensuring the continued viability and relevance of learning and training programmes also calls for the regular review of programmes. As the findings of the OECD Survey highlight, though this is occurring, it needs to be made more systematic and linked to other inputs such as the regular review of government priorities and the results of evaluations.

Schools of government are also under pressure to respond to the changing needs for civil service skills and the requirements of governments, in light of new citizen expectations and policy priorities. As such regular programme review and alignment would help ensure that schools' offerings of learning and development programmes address the main areas where skills gaps have been identified. This also requires schools to develop the means to effectively assess and identify the skills gaps that need to be filled.

Finally, schools of government with research programmes tend to focus mainly on applied research in the areas that are broadly consistent with government priorities. At the same time, the link between the research and learning and training programmes still needs to be clarified. This will help ensure that the research is focused and contributes to learning activities, while learning programmes remain topical and relevant.

In light of the above, schools of government may consider the following recommendations:

- **Recommendation 3.1**: Regularly review schools' learning and development programmes to ensure that both the content and delivery methods are best suited to meeting the needs of learners and governments.
- **Recommendation 3.2**: Assess the scope for introducing innovative techniques in the delivery and content of learning and development, including the use of social media and other information and communications technologies.
- **Recommendation 3.3**: Strengthen the link between research and knowledge development activities and learning programmes. This will ensure that learning programmes remain relevant and up to date with changing government priorities and emerging social, economic and political trends.

Notes

1. Applied research is a methodology used to solve a specific, practical problem of an individual or group.

References

Australian Government (2013), "Australian Public Service induction", Australian Public Service Commission, www.apsc.gov.au/working-in-the-aps/apsinduction.

Boud, D. and P. Hager (2011), "Re-thinking continuing professional development through changing metaphors and location in professional practice", *Studies in Continuing Education,* 34(1), pp. 17-30, http://dx.doi.org/10.1080/0158037X.2011.608656.

CIPD (Chartered Institute of Personnel and Development) (2016), "Factsheets: Induction programmes", www.cipd.co.uk/hr-resources/factsheets/induction.aspx.

CSPS (Canada School of Public Service) (2015), "On-line courses", www.csps-efpc.gc.ca/.

Goldsmith, M. and L. Carter (2009), *Best Practices in Talent Management: How the World's Leading Corprations Develop and Retain Top Talent*, Wiley, London.

National Education Association (2013), "NEA Policy Statement on Digital Learning", National Education Association, www.nea.org/home/55434.htm.

OECD (forthcoming), "National Schools of Government Network Annual Meeting 2016: Summary report", OECD.

OECD (2014), "2014 OECD Survey of National Schools of Government".

OECD (2010), "Human Resources Management: Country Profiles", webpage, www.oecd.org/gov/pem/hrpractices.htm.

OECD (1997), "Public Service Training in OECD Countries", *SIGMA Papers*, No. 16, OECD Publishing, Paris, http://dx.doi.org/10.1787/5kml619ljzzn-en.

Rosenbaum, Allan (ed.) (2015), *In Quest of Excellence: Approaches to Enhancing the Quality of Public Administration Education and Training*, NISPAcee, Slovensko.

UK Government (2014), "Civil Service: Training and development (Guidance)", www.gov.uk/guidance/training-and-development-opportunities-in-the-the-civil-service.

Victoria State Government (2015), "Using Digital Technologies to Support Learning and Teaching", *School Policy and Advisory Guide*, Victoria State Government: Education and Training, www.education.vic.gov.au/school/principals/spag/curriculum/pages/techsupport.aspx.

de Vries, M. (2014), "International Accreditation of PA Programs: Narrations of an Evaluator", *The NISPAcee Journal of Public Administration and Policy*, Vol. VI, No. 2, www.degruyter.com/downloadpdf/j/nispa.2013.6.issue-2/nispa-2013-0008/nispa-2013-0008.pdf.

Chapter 4

Evaluating the success of national schools of government

This chapter outlines and explores different approaches that schools of government use as ways to assess whether they are effectively maintaining and enhancing the quality of public administration education and training. The evaluation of learning activities has attracted increased attention in recent years in the context of reduced resources. The evaluation approaches aim at meeting citizens' need to ensure that learning and development programmes are delivering value for money and have a positive impact upon public service delivery. An understanding of the political, social and economic contextual factors that shape educational programmes and their potential for producing desired outcomes is viewed as essential in assessing quality. The chapter looks into alternatives to current evaluation approaches.

Introduction

Ensuring that schools of government (or "schools") respond to government needs and priorities calls for robust monitoring and evaluation. The evaluation of learning activities has attracted increased attention in recent years in the context of reduced resources and the need to ensure that learning and development programmes are delivering value for money. There is growing recognition that schools' course and programme evaluations can contribute to:

- **Improving training current and future training**: Evaluation feedback and data on participants' impressions of training or other developmental activities can drive continuous improvement. This applies to training as much as other developmental activities.
- **Confirming the relevance and value of the programmes and that these are meeting the needs of the target clientele**: Evaluation can also be used to ensure that training and development programmes are effectively equipping staff with the right skills and knowledge needed to fulfil their duties. This can further ensure that investments in training are meeting actual needs and aligned with business objectives.
- **Demonstrating value, as an accountability measure**: Training and development can represent a significant expense for public organisations and, as a consequence, there is increasing expectation to demonstrate the value added, especially in periods where resources become tighter. Evaluation data can therefore be an important source of information on which to base future training and development budget allocations.

Yet, like many other training and educational institutions, schools of government often face difficulties in evaluating the outcomes of their training and development initiatives, often framed as acquired competencies of current and future civil servants. Though nearly 90% of schools reported seeking the input of learners to evaluate their courses and programmes, the impact of training was assessed by less than 10% of respondents to the 2014 OECD Survey of National Schools of Government (or "OECD Survey") (see Figure 4.1).

For the most part, the principal means by which schools evaluated their courses consisted in the use of use of participant satisfaction surveys (used by 85% of survey respondents). This may in part be explained by the relative ease of use, low complexity, and low cost of participant surveys.

Some 50% of OECD Survey respondents reported using other means of evaluation, such as feedback cards. The most in-depth forms of evaluations reported included regular evaluations, though responses were not specific about how these were used. Moreover, these methods do not permit in-depth evaluation of factors such as the extent to which newly acquired knowledge or skills are applied in day-to-day practice, or result in behavioural change. These factors can only be assessed at some distance in time from the training.

Figure 4.1. **Modes and methods of evaluation of national schools of government activities**

Q. As your school monitors and evaluates its activities, how does it monitor and evaluate their impact?

Source: OECD (2014), "2014 OECD Survey of National Schools of Government".

Importantly, collecting learner impressions of courses and programmes is only one part of the overall evaluation and monitoring that is needed to determine the performance of schools as institutions. Nearly all respondents (93%) reported having in place monitoring and evaluation processes to evaluate the effectiveness of their programmes and teaching methods in order to demonstrate both value for money and the contribution made by schools to government priorities and delivery, especially in a context of diminishing resources. This was followed by course inputs and outputs evaluation (assessed by 57% of respondents). Other areas of evaluation concerned areas oriented toward the general performance of the institution, such as the assessment of their efficiency and cost-effectiveness.

In some OECD countries, governments have used staff surveys to determine the impact of learning and training options (see Box 4.1). These evaluation methods measure the immediate impressions of participants, and as such, may be of limited utility to assess impacts and outcomes of learning. Lessons learned from these surveys show the necessity for schools to undertake more comprehensive evaluations of their programmes than is currently the case. It does not appear that schools are actively evaluating the outcomes and impacts of their programmes. While actively soliciting learner reactions in the immediate aftermath of their learning programme, few schools undertake evaluations with the purpose of measuring their programmes as contributing to employee effectiveness upon their completion on their jobs.

Box 4.1. Public service staff satisfaction surveys

In some countries (e.g. Australia, Canada, the United Kingdom and the United States) public service staff are asked for their impressions of the training and development they have received. For example, results from the Australia Public Service Employee Census showed that 72% of employees rated their learning and development as moderately effective in helping to improve their work performance (and in 28% of cases training was felt to be highly or very highly effective) (Australian Public Service Commission, 2014, p. 161).

In the case of Canada, the results of the Public Service Employee Survey that in the six years between the 2008 and 2014 employee surveys the perception of the training received and its contribution to job performance remained relatively stable at 63% of respondents in 2014 as compared to 69% in 2011 and 68% in 2008 (Treasury Board Secretariat, 2014).

In the United Kingdom, 51% of respondents to the 2014 Civil Service People Survey indicated that the training they had received in the last 12 months had helped them be better at their jobs. By contrast, 72 % of the senior civil service said that the training they had received had helped them be better at their job (Cabinet Office, 2014, p. 4).

In the United States, the results of the 2015 Federal Employee Viewpoint Survey show that across all job categories, 52 % of staff were satisfied with the training received for their present job, a figure essentially unchanged since 2012 (Office of Personnel Management, 2015, p. 22).

Looking ahead, schools may consider undertaking a broader range of surveys, which can also be used to assess the impact of training on behavioural changes, especially for staff in direct service delivery roles to the public or internally, such as through the use of satisfaction surveys. Other methods could include involving the civil service personnel management function by assigning to them the role of gathering training and staff performance information as a means of determining whether training has had any impact (Wilcox Johnson, n.d.; Phillips, 2010).

Several models already in use in the higher education field could serve as the templates for impact evaluations of learning and training programmes. For example, Ireland's Institute of Public Administration assesses the relevance of its programmes through the National Framework of Qualifications (NFQs) (see Box 4.2). The NFQs establish a comparative basis focused on learning outcomes for learners on the basis of a given qualification (Quality and Qualifications Ireland, 2015). The use of NFQs further establishes benchmarks that can be used in the comparative assessment of institutional performance. Another example of a comprehensive approach to evaluating the quality of its educational programmes used by France's ENA is highlighted in Box 4.3. ENA's approach highlights the importance of collecting and using comprehensive indicators to assess the performance and quality of a programme – from inputs (e.g. invested resources), activities (e.g. organisation of work, efficiency such as cost per unit) to outputs (e.g. quality of teaching) and outcomes (e.g. acquired competencies). The development of such a holistic approach could be facilitated by the logic model, which would spell out the theory underlying a programme and help frame questions about programme implementation and outcomes.

Box 4.2. Ireland's National Framework of Qualifications

Qualifications frameworks describe the qualifications of an education and training system and how they interlink. National qualifications frameworks describe what learners should know, understand and be able to do on the basis of a given qualification. These frameworks also show how learners can move from one qualification, or qualification level, to another within a system. Over 150 countries are now developing, or have developed, a national qualifications framework.

The Irish NFQ, established in 2003, is a framework through which all learning achievements may be measured and related to each other in a coherent way. The many different types and sizes of qualifications included in the NFQ are organised based on their level of knowledge, skill and competence. Because all NFQ qualifications are quality assured, learners can be confident that they will be recognised at home and abroad.

Quality and Qualifications Ireland (QQI) has responsibility to develop, promote and maintain the Irish NFQ.

Source: Quality and Qualifications Ireland (2015), "National Framework of Qualifications (NFQ)", www.qqi.ie/Pages/National-Framework-of-Qualifications-(NFQ).aspx.

Box 4.3. ENA's approach to evaluation and quality improvement

ENA's quality assessment programme covers a range of interventions which includes several methods such as self-assessment, peer-review, quality reports and a satisfaction survey. Various monitoring and evaluation measures are integrated in a thorough system of comprehensive, systematic and continuous quality control. Quality control starts with the use of very restrictive criteria when selecting the candidates who will take part in the 27 month training course.

This first step is completed by different forms of quality controls conducted during the program. In order to make sure that the content of the training program matches the students' needs in terms of specific knowledge and skills, individual student interviews are organised at different times: at the very outset regarding their expectations; at mid-term in order to know whether they need special support to gain maximum benefit from the courses; and at the end of the programme through interviews with human resource management experts to help them better identify which skills and competences they have and to which tasks and jobs they are best suited. ENA's principal responsibility is to recruit and train the men and women who will make public service a living institution and enable it to adapt to ever-changing times. Professional training at ENA means that most of the teachers are high level practitioners, experts in their field of activity.

At the end of each class, students fill in individual evaluation forms on the teacher's performance and the relevance of the course. At the same time, students' representatives supply the training department with students' feed-back regarding the perceived quality and appropriateness of the curriculum. Half of the training program consists of internships (so called "stages") in different administrations, where the students are in charge of very demanding tasks with a high level of responsibility. The reports drafted by the supervisors provide not only evaluation on the students' performances but also useful information on the actual levels of the students' progress and possible shortcomings in the training program. Thus, they give information on whether or not the students are ready and capable to cope with their future tasks.

Box 4.3. ENA's approach to evaluation and quality improvement *(continued)*

In a third step, one quality control procedure carried out at ENA is ex-post evaluations and impact assessment conducted either informally via exchanges with, and feed-back gained from, the powerful association of ENA alumni. The alumni are not just former students of the school. They are also the employers or colleagues of the new graduates. Their feedback also provides an understanding of whether the current profile and qualifications of the newcomers match the tasks to be performed and the challenges to be met in today's public administration. More formally and systematically conducted are the yearly surveys based on questionnaires sent to all the graduates who left ENA in the past 14 months and who started to work in the French public administration. A parallel questionnaire is sent to their supervisors in the ministries and agencies where they work in order to get insights on whether the content of the training provided at ENA meets the expectations and needs of French public administration and whether the former students feel they have been well prepared to carry out their duty.

In [final] stage, information gained at different levels and stages is carefully analysed by the training department who may consider adapting or modifying the organisation of the curriculum and the design of the syllabus, the balance between different pedagogical tools, the content of some courses, as well as the decision whether or not to employ again the teachers who were asked to contribute to the training programme.

Source: Larat, F. (2015), "Internal and external quality control mechanisms: Lessons drawn from the Ecole Nationale d'Administration", in Rosenbaum Allan (ed.) (2015), *In Quest of Excellence: Approaches to Enhancing the Quality of Public Administration Education and Training*. Slovensko: NISPAcee,

While most of the schools actively evaluate their learning programmes, it is rare that they evaluate their research activities. On the whole, this finding is not surprising given the difficulty associated with evaluating policy research programmes (Nason and O'Neill, 2015). However, as research activities are also subject to demonstrating their value for money, this may also prove to be an area in which schools may need to undertake further effort.

In terms of the evaluation actors, in approximately 30% of instances the evaluation of schools' performance was undertaken internally by either the Board of Directors (in 29% of responses to the OECD Survey) or by the institution's senior management (in 43% of responses). Looking ahead, the schools may benefit from greater investment in independent evaluations to ensure full objectivity and focus on impacts. Such evaluations can also be part of the accreditation process (as applicable) or assessment of programme quality.

Overall, as shown in Table 4.1, the three most frequently cited success factors for schools were the quality or relevance of their programme or courses, the existence of a policy on learning and training, and an integrated training strategy. These findings, especially the importance of the quality and relevance of schools' activities, underline the need for comprehensive monitoring and evaluations strategies. Furthermore these findings suggest that there is considerable scope for schools to develop evaluation processes to assess the worth, effectiveness, and success or failure of learning and programme outcomes (Menix, 2007).

Table 4.1. **National schools of government success factors**

Q. What do you think were the three most important factors contributing to the success of the school?

	Programme/course quality, relevance	A "whole-of-government" learning/training strategy	A specific legislation/policy on civil service learning/training	Effective accountability mechanisms for civil service learning/training	Co-ordination mechanisms across levels of government	Co-ordination mechanisms across departments/ministries	A "whole-of-government" research programme	Monitoring and evaluation	Other
Australia	①	③			②				
Austria	①		②	③					
Belgium	①	③					②		
Brazil	①	②	③						
Canada	②		①						③[2]
Egypt	①			③				②	
France	①	③	②						
Greece[1]	②	①	②					③	
Hungary	①				③			②	
Ireland	①	②						③	
Italy	①	②					③		
Lebanon	①					③			②[3]
Luxembourg	②					①		③	
Mexico	③	②						①	
Netherlands	①	③	②						
Philippines	①		②			③			
Poland					①	②		③	
Russia	①		②						
Slovenia	②	①	③						
Spain	①		③			②			
Ukraine	①		②						③[4]
United Kingdom	①		③	②					

Notes:

1. Greece combines responses from both EKDDA and INERP.

2. Senior-level support in the public service of the strategic value of the school.

3. Ministerial support and endorsement; Organisational framework of the school.

4. Leadership and vision.

Source: OECD (2014), "2014 OECD Survey of National Schools of Government".

More broadly, schools are under pressure to demonstrate return on investment in education, which is often a challenge given the diffused way that potential benefits may manifest themselves. In this context, the risk is that during difficult financial periods, training and development programmes are likely to be cut among the first ones if they are not able to demonstrate clear measurable outcomes. OECD work on higher education more broadly showed that returns on investment can be rather significant (Box 4.4 and Figure 4.2). Some schools are taking steps to deepen the understanding of the impact of their activities. For examples, ANZGOC recently started a longitudinal study of the career trajectories of its graduates – before, during and after the relevant programme, which could help deepen the analysis of the return on investment in the area of public leadership and administration.

Box 4.4. What are the returns on investment in higher education?

- On average across 25 OECD countries, the long-term economic advantage to an individual of having a tertiary degree instead of an upper secondary degree is over USD 175 000 for a man and USD 110 000 for a woman.
- The long-term economic advantage to individuals with a tertiary education is about twice as large as the advantage for people with an upper secondary education as their highest educational level, on average across OECD countries.
- The net return to taxpayers on the public costs of supporting a man in higher education is over USD 91 000, and the return for supporting a woman in higher education is over USD 55 000, on average across OECD countries.
- On average, OECD countries directly invest more than USD 30 000 in public sector funds to support an individual pursuing higher education. This includes taxpayer funds used to reduce the direct costs of higher education to individuals and support for grant and loan programs. Foregone tax revenues and social contributions while individuals are in education represent additional indirect costs.
- Evidence shows that over the long run, however, countries will recoup this investment – through increased tax revenues from the higher-educated people, savings from the lower level of social transfers these individuals typically receive. For example, the net return on the public costs to support a man in tertiary education is more than USD 91 000, on average across OECD countries – more than three times the amount of the public investment.

Source: OECD (2012), "Education Indicators in Focus", www.oecd.org/edu/skills-beyond-school/Education%20Indicators%20in%20Focus%206%20June%202012.pdf .

Figure 4.2. **Private costs and benefits for a man obtaining higher education (in USD, 2007 or latest available year)**

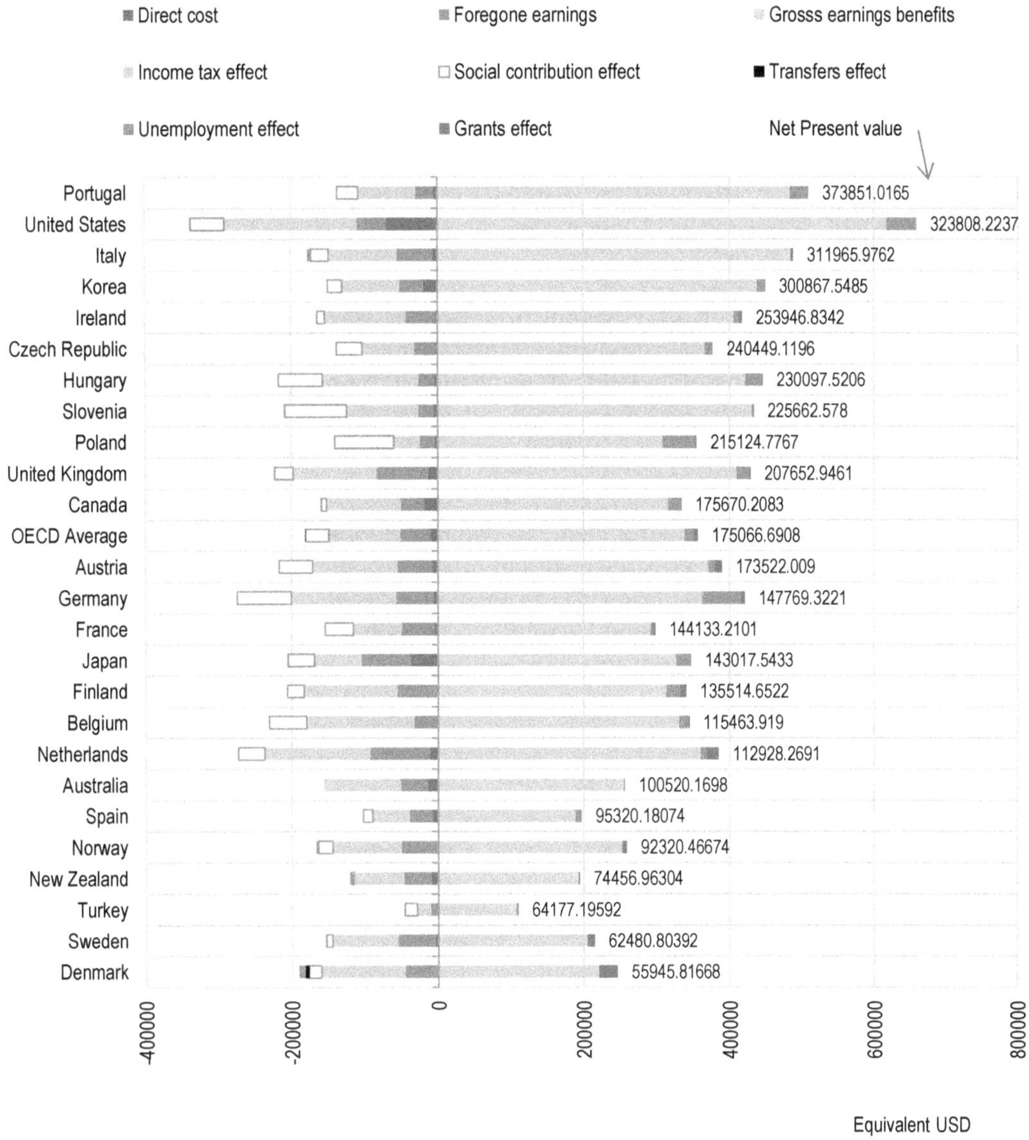

Direct cost
Foregone earnings
Grosss earnings benefits
Income tax effect
Social contribution effect
Transfers effect
Unemployment effect
Grants effect
Net Present value

Portugal 373851.0165
United States 323808.2237
Italy 311965.9762
Korea 300867.5485
Ireland 253946.8342
Czech Republic 240449.1196
Hungary 230097.5206
Slovenia 225662.578
Poland 215124.7767
United Kingdom 207652.9461
Canada 175670.2083
OECD Average 175066.6908
Austria 173522.009
Germany 147769.3221
France 144133.2101
Japan 143017.5433
Finland 135514.6522
Belgium 115463.919
Netherlands 112928.2691
Australia 100520.1698
Spain 95320.18074
Norway 92320.46674
New Zealand 74456.96304
Turkey 64177.19592
Sweden 62480.80392
Denmark 55945.81668

-400000 -200000 0 200000 400000 600000 800000

Equivalent USD

Notes:

Australia, Belgium and Turkey refer to 2005; Italy, the Netherlands, Poland, Portugal and the United Kingdom refer to 2006. All other countries refer to 2007.

Cash flows are discounted at a 3% interest rate.

Countries are ranked in descending order of the net present value.

Source: OECD (2011), *Education at a Glance 2011: OECD Indicators*, OECD Publishing, Paris, http://dx.doi.org/10.1787/eag-2011-en.

Assessment and recommendations

It has long been recognised that learning and training programmes need to be evaluated for their effectiveness. Positive evaluation feedback from learners and other key stakeholders in government can serve to confirm the content, design and delivery of training programmes. However, evaluation results – both positive and negative – also contribute to the process of review and renewal. For example, evaluations enable the assessment the learning programmes contribution to the attainment of organisational objectives, the value of maintaining these programmes, insights into their improvement, or areas where new programmes may be needed (Kirkpatrick and Kirkpatrick, 2009).

For the most part, schools of government appear to be aware of the benefits of evaluation and have in place evaluation and monitoring mechanisms that are in keeping with approaches used across the field of professional training. Most of these are internally managed, however, and are carried out using traditional methods, such as participant surveys. Some schools are beginning to analyse the return on investment in their programmes.

This being said, in an environment in which government institutions must increasingly demonstrate their effectiveness and efficiency, there is an opportunity for schools to strengthen their monitoring and evaluation practices. This can be done by conducting evaluations of all their activities, including research, in order to demonstrate how these contribute to institutional and governments' goals and priorities. Doing so may require schools to move toward independent evaluations that are based on an extended range of tools and inputs. The results of evaluations should also be integrated into the process of planning, design, and delivery of existing and new learning offerings.

Looking to the future, schools could consider evaluating their offerings, not just with learners, but also with organisations, such as through *ex post* evaluations of employee performance management. Though several examples of training impacts were discussed above, in the future, schools could gain the ability to conduct these types of evaluations.

Evaluations are also important for research programmes conducted by the schools. Recognising the difficulty involved in measuring the effectiveness and results of research activities is a challenge across the civil service. However, schools may consider models used in the academic sphere to evaluate research activities and impact, though these would need to be adapted to their operating contexts.

In light of the above, schools of government may consider the following recommendations:

- **Recommendation 4.1**: Expand the use of comprehensive evaluations of their learning programme effectiveness, with particular attention to the worth, impact, and success of programme outcomes. Particular attention should be given to assessing the impact of learning programmes on employee and organisational effectiveness and performance, including return on investment in education.
- **Recommendation 4.2**: Consider alternatives to current evaluation methods for the purpose of increasing the breadth, scope and type of programme evaluations. Enhance the use of independent evaluations.

- **Recommendation 4.3**: Consider evaluations of their research and knowledge development activities with particular attention paid to their integration in learning programmes and their impact on institutional and government priorities.

References

Australian Public Service Commission (2014), *State of the Service Report: State of the Services Series 2013-2014*, Australian Public Service Commission, Canberra.

Cabinet Office (2014), *Civil Service People Survey 2014*, Cabinet Office, London, United Kingdom.

Kirkpatrick, D. and J. Kirkpatrick (2009), *Evaluating Training Programs*, Berrett-Koehler Publishers.

Larat, F., "Internal and External Quality Control mechanisms: Lessons Drawn from the Ecole Nationale d'Administration" in Rosenbaum Allan (ed.) (2015), *In Quest of Excellence: Approaches to Enhancing the Quality of Public Administration Education and Training*, NISPAcee, Slovensko.

Menix, K.D. (2007), "Evaluation of learning and program effectiveness", *J Contin Educ Nurs,* 38(5), pp. 201-8.

Nason, E. and M. O'Neill (2015), "What metrics? On the utility of measuring the performance of policy research: An illustrative case and alternative from Employment and Social Development Canada", *Canadian Public Administration*, *58*(1), pp. 138-160.

OECD (2014), "2014 OECD Survey of National Schools of Government".

OECD (2011), *Education at a Glance 2011: OECD Indicators*, OECD Publishing, Paris, http://dx.doi.org/10.1787/eag-2011-en.

Office of Personnel Management (2015), "Federal Employee Viewpoint Survey Results: Employees Influencing Change - Governmentwide Management Report", Office of Personnel Management, Washington.

Phillips, P. (2010), *Measuring and Evaluating Training*, ATD Press, Alexandria, VA.

Rosenbaum, A., (ed.) (2015), *In Quest of Excellence: Approaches to Enhancing the Quality of Public Administration Education and Training*, NISPAcee, Slovensko.

Quality and Qualifications Ireland (2015), "National Framework of Qualifications (NFQ)", www.qqi.ie/Pages/National-Framework-of-Qualifications-(NFQ).aspx.

Treasury Board Secretariat (2014), "Highlights: 2014 Public Service Employee Survey", Treasury Board Secretariat, Ottawa, www.tbs-sct.gc.ca/psm-fpfm/modernizing-modernisation/pses-saff/hlr-rfs-eng.asp.

Wilcox Johnson, D. (n.d.), "Evaluating training", *Thinking Outside the Borders*, pp. 17-23.

Chapter 5

National schools of government: Building relationships and co-ordination

This chapter considers the institutional foundations of the schools of government and their relationship to government, as well as the means by which schools co-ordinate their activities with other government and non-governmental institutions. The chapter suggests that greater engagement is necessary to bridge the gap between curricula and practice. In particular, it examines the relationships of schools of government with the government and other institutional stakeholders. Finally, the chapter also looks into the internal governance and management of the schools and how this may influence their mandate, activities and capacity to respond to government priorities.

Introduction

Institutional forms and relationships tend have an important impact on the ability of schools of government (or "schools") to design and deliver effective, efficient and responsive programmes that take into account the needs and priorities of individual learners, support the government agenda and also equip the government with the skills and knowledge to deal with uncertainty and future priorities. To this end, this chapter provides an overview of the institutional models of different schools of government that have been adopted to support civil service learning. In particular, it examines the presence of schools of government, their relationships with the government and other institutional stakeholders, as well as their internal management and governance arrangements. The chapter further explores the impact of various institutional dimensions on schools' capacity to respond to government priorities.

Schools as national learning and development organisations

There is a wide range of institutional choices made by OECD and partner countries and economies in providing and supporting civil service learning. As shown in Figure 5.1, all of the respondents to the 2014 OECD Survey of National Schools of Government (or "OECD Survey") reported having an institution responsible for civil service learning in place, although they differed in their institutional form, mandate and relationship to government.

Figure 5.1. **Presence of governmental training institutions in selected countries**

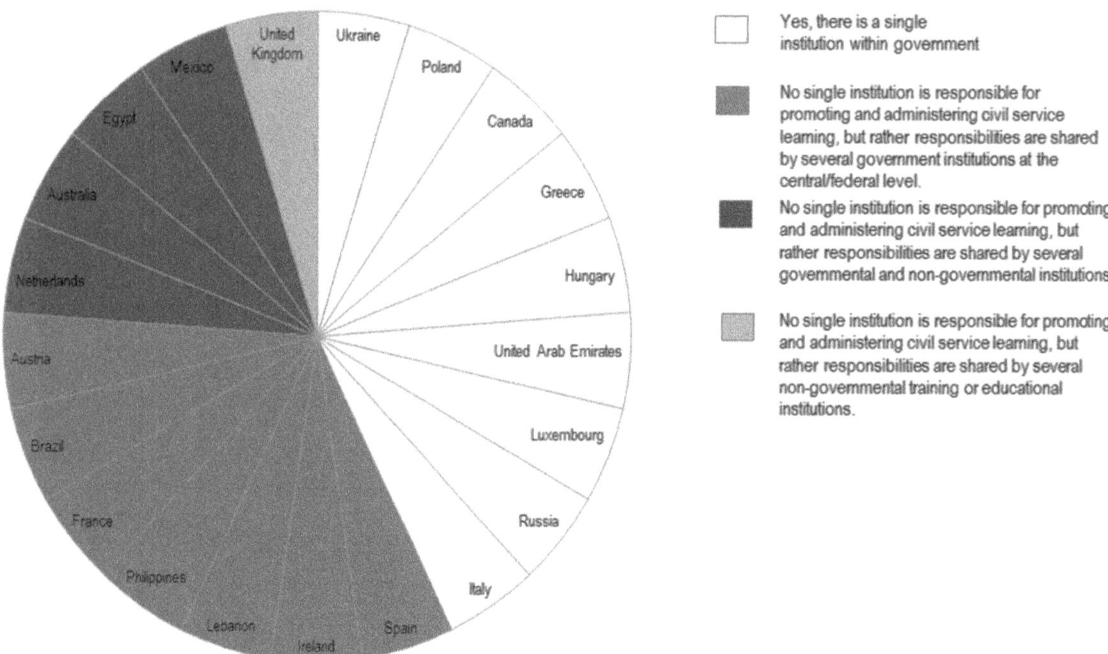

Source: OECD (2014a), "2014 OECD Survey of National Schools of Government".

The breakdown of the responses is as follows:

- **A single institution within government**: Ten responding countries reported having a single institution within government, although there is considerable variance in their institutional structure and organisation. These are: Ukraine, Poland, Canada, Spain, Greece, Hungary, United Arab Emirates, Luxembourg, Russia and Italy. Among these, several countries have established a single national government institution for civil service training (Ukraine, Poland, Canada, Spain, Greece, Luxembourg, Russia, and Italy). In the case of the United Arab Emirates and Hungary these roles are held by post-secondary education institutions. With the exception of Canada, Poland, Luxembourg and Italy, all are degree-granting institutions.
- **Shared responsibility across government:** Six countries reported that the responsibilities are shared by several government institutions at the central level. These are: Austria, Brazil, France, Philippines, Lebanon and Ireland. For example, in Ireland, civil service training is provided by Ireland's Institute of Public Administration, the Civil Service Training and Development Centre (CSTDC) and individual departments and agencies (Civil Service Training and Development, 2011). Only in France and Lebanon are these degree-granting institutions.
- **Shared responsibility with non-governmental stakeholders**: Of the responding countries, the responsibilities are shared between governmental and non-governmental institutions in four. These include: Mexico, Egypt, Australia, and the Netherlands. Of these, the schools in Mexico and Australia are degree-granting institutions.[1] The Australia New Zealand School of Government (ANZSOG) is a non-governmental, not-for-profit institution with a civil service training mandate.[2] ANZSOG's is unique among survey respondents as it was established by two national governments, nine Australian state and territorial governments, and sixteen member universities. Government members contribute approximately 8% of its income and contribute actively to its activities and development (ANZSOG, n.d.). Another 14 Australian and New Zealand governmental and non-governmental institutions also partner with ANZSOG on specific programmes. These partner institutions include national and state bodies, such as New Zealand's State Services Commission, Queensland Department of Prime Minister and Cabinet and the OECD. One country, the United Kingdom, noted that training and development responsibilities are shared by several non-governmental training or educational institutions, meaning that civil service learning had been outsourced to a non-governmental private institution. This is the case for the United Kingdom's Civil Service College (Civil Service College, 2016; OECD, 2014a). The Civil Service College does not grant degrees.

Overall, such institutional arrangements tend to be linked to the type of national civil service system – career-based, position-based or mixed (see Table 5.1). While these are increasingly mixed, schools of government established in countries with career-based systems tend to offer initial and flexible training focused on career development (e.g. France, Germany). Such training can be less important for position-based systems (e.g. United Kingdom) as the emphasis is on recruiting specialists with a certain set of skills for a particular position.

Table 5.1. **Civil service systems and civil service training institutions**

Civil service system	Civil service training institution	Example
Position-based system	National schools of government / Academy of public service	Slovenia (Academy)
	Private sector or non-governmental	United Kingdom (Civil Service Learning)
	Universities or other institutions of tertiary education	Australia (ANZSOG), New Zealand (ANZSOG)
Position-based system combining career-based system elements	National schools of government / Academy of public service	Canada (CSPS), Mexico (INAP), Austria (FAPS), Ireland (IPA), Poland (NSPA),Hungary (NUPS), Russia (RANEPA)
Career-based system	National schools of government / Academy of public service	Italy (SNA), France (ENA), Spain (INAP) , Greece (IMERP/HNCPA), Slovak Republic (MPA)
	Universities or other institutions of tertiary education	United Arab Emirates (MBRSG)

Source: Author own work based on ReSPA (Regional School of Public Administration) (2008), *Civil Service Training Systems in the Western Balkans Region*, ReSPA, Montenegro and OECD (2010), "Human Resources Management: Country Profiles", www.oecd.org/gov/pem/hrpractices.htm.

These different institutional models have in some cases emerged as a result of considerable organisational changes, in particular through the consolidation of learning under a single institutional umbrella. Some of the reasons for this consolidation include the aim to:

- provide civil servants with integrated learning across the civil service
- provide a uniform approach to learning in certain key areas, such as leadership, which is not tied to particular functional categories
- reduce administrative barriers and reduce costs
- support a single government-wide policy for learning through a single institutional delivery point.

Three examples of recent consolidations are presented in Box 5.1.

Box 5.1. **Examples of consolidation in civil service training institutions in Canada, Hungary and Italy**

Canada School of Public Service (CSPS)

CSPS was created on 1 April 2004 as the main training and professional development for the Government of Canada. CSPS is the successor organisation to the Canadian Centre for Management Development (CCMD) (established in 1991) and results from the amalgamation of CCMD, Training and Development Canada and Language Training Canada. The latter two bodies existed as administrative units within the Department of Public Works and Government Services.

Though CSPS was established as a central institution for civil training for the whole of the Canadian government, departments are empowered to deliver training to their staff and some departments have retained or established their own training capacities relevant to their mandates, such as the Department of Foreign Affairs, International Trade and Development and Service Canada.

Box 5.1. Examples of consolidation in civil service training institutions in Canada, Hungary and Italy *(continued)*

Hungary's National University of Public Service (Nemzeti Közszolgálati Egyetem, NUPS)

Officially established on 1 January 2012, NUPS can trace its institutional heritage over 200 years. Formed through the amalgamation of the Zrínyi Miklós National Defence University, the Police College and the Faculty of Public Administration, Corvinus University of Budapest, the history of these institutions link NUPS with the development of the Hungarian State:

- the College of Public Administration, founded in 1977 (later renamed the Faculty of Public Administration, Corvinus University of Budapest, in 2005)
- the Police College, founded in 1970
- Zrínyi Miklós National Defence University, founded in 1996, itself the continuation of the Royal Hungarian Ludovika Academy, established in 1808.

Italy's National School of Administration (Scola Nazionale dell Ádministrazione, SNA)

Founded in 1957 the National School of Administration (SNA) amalgamated in 2004 the responsibilities for training that had been provided by the five civil service academies in the ministries of Economy and Finance, Foreign Affairs, Interior, Defence (civil staff), and National Institute of Statistics.

Sources: Author's own work based on country responses to OECD (2014a), "2014 OECD Survey of National Schools of Government" and publicly available sources.

These choices of institutional models also highlight different policy choices between the centralisation and decentralisation of civil service training. Though there is no one-size-fits-all model, it is important to keep in mind the institutional consequences for each approach. Dividing responsibility for training among several agencies may result in fragmented and inconsistent programmes and may place an increasing emphasis on the need to co-ordinate. Centralising civil service learning and development activities may result in training services becoming too far removed from the demand and, as such, may require greater efforts for priority identification (such as skills needs) and impact evaluation. However, irrespective of the model chosen, greater effectiveness can often be achieved by ensuring that the agencies adopt common policies on civil service learning (OECD, 2014b, p. 42).

It is also important to note that even when civil service learning and development activities are offered by schools that are not institutions of government, as for example in the case of ANZSOG or Singapore's the Lee Kwan Yew School, a formal link with government is a common feature (see Box 5.2). Thus in 88% of cases, non-governmental respondents to the OECD Survey stated that they had a formal arrangement, or an affiliation existed with a government institution linked to their training mission.

Box 5.2. Australia New Zealand School of Government (ANZSOG)

ANZSOG was established in 2002 as a unique initiative of governments, universities and business schools.

Australian and New Zealand governments recognised the need for a world-class centre to provide tailored learning opportunities for future civil service leaders. ANZSOG's ultimate purpose is to achieve better outcomes for society by enhancing the civil service's capacity for good public policy and effective administration. In doing so, the school plays a key role in promoting public service as a profession of great social value.

The school has several distinctive features:

- A collaborative partnership between governments and universities, which ensures all course offerings are academically rigorous and directly applicable to civil service requirements. Collaboration across jurisdictions also facilitates a focus on common problems.
- A networked delivery model, with teaching and research drawing on the strengths of member universities in Australia and New Zealand, as well as the best academics and practitioners internationally.
- An emphasis on building strategic and "adaptive" management capacity, including the ability to deliver public value in challenging settings.
- A commitment to the best in teaching that recognises the specific needs of experienced executives draws upon their knowledge and translates into immediate application in the workplace.
- Programme cohorts selected for their potential to attain positions of high-level leadership and management, and for their commitment to public service.

Source: ANZSOG (Australia New Zealand School of Government) (n.d), "About ANZSOG", www.anzsog.edu.au/ and www.anzsog.edu.au/about-us/about-anzsog (accessed 6 August 2016).

Some factors may account for the different modes of delivery, including:

- economic and fiscal capacity (i.e. reflecting choice and capacity of government fund the activities or seek alternative modes of funding such as fee for service or public-private-partnership arrangements)
- institutional autonomy (i.e. where activities include academic or quasi-academic activities)
- institutional attachment to centre of government (i.e. where activities contribute to the definition or realisation of government priorities)
- mandate flexibility (i.e. where institutional design accounts for the need to adapt to evolving priorities of government or other key stakeholders)
- clientele (i.e. whole-of-civil-service or focus on management cadre).

Institutional framework of schools of government

The choice of institutional model may also have an impact on the relationships between the schools and government institutions. As illustrated in Figure 5.2, three types of institutional relationships exist between schools of government and other institutions of government.

Figure 5.2. **Models of institutional relationships between schools of government and other government institutions**

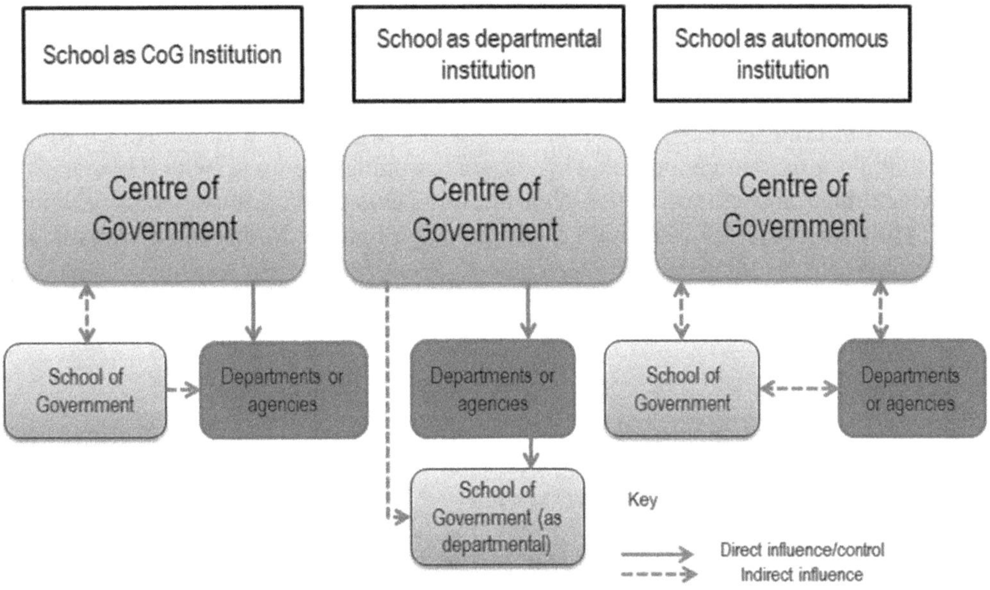

Source: Author's own work.

In the first model, the school is institutionally situated within or close to the centre of government (CoG), which may serve as an indicator of the importance given to civil service training as a core government mission. Situated within the CoG, the schools respond directly to the training priorities that are identified by the CoG. Other government bodies are also subject to the same degree of CoG direction. Considered from another perspective, the closer to the CoG a school is situated, the greater the influence the CoG will have on the definition of learning needs and priorities. For schools this proximity may be advantageous as it may increase its capacity to translate government priorities into learning and development programmes, and reciprocally influence the learning priorities for the whole of government. This may be critical in the determination of civil service training. Among OECD Survey respondents, 25% (7 out of 24 respondents) reported an institutional relationship with a CoG institution. Countries with this institutional model include: Austria, Hungary,[3] Italy, Poland, Russia, and United Arab Emirates.[4] For example, Italy's SNA is part of the Office of the Prime Minister. In 35% of cases (11 out of 24 respondents) the relationship was with a ministry responsible for public administration, as for example, in the case of Mexico,[5] Ukraine[6] and Spain's INAP.

In the second type of relationship, the school is an institution within the portfolio of another government department or agency. In this model the training priorities of government are communicated to the department and, in turn, transmitted to the school. In this model the school may have more or less administrative and policy autonomy from the lead portfolio department. Moreover, if they possess a mandate to provide training across all of government, they may also have to be responsive to the CoG direction, though possibly with some degree of latitude from CoG direction. In the case of 25% of OECD Survey respondents (7 out of 24 surveyed institutions), the principal relations was with a civil service ministry or human resources agency. Countries with this institutional model include: Brazil, Canada, Ireland, Lebanon, Luxembourg,[7] Slovenia and Spain. For example, the Canada School of Public Service is part of the portfolio responsible for civil service human resources policy (OECD, 2014a, Q. 36). As shown in Table 5.2, few OECD Survey respondents identified relationships with institutions captured in the "other" category. In instances where the relationships existed with institutions other than the CoG or ministries of public administration or civil services, these relationships are principally with ministries with specific training programme needs. This is for example the case with Hungary's NUPS, which maintains extensive ties with the ministries of the Interior, Justice, and Defence. The relationship of the NUPS is one of subordination to these ministries and the Office of the Prime Minister.

Table 5.2. **National schools of government institutional relationships**

Q. Please indicate the nature of the relationship and co-ordination arrangements

	Centre of Government	Ministry of public administration or its equivalent	Civil Service Ministry or its equivalent that is responsible for the HRM of civil service	Other Government institutions
Brazil		●		
Canada			❍	
France		●		
Greece (INERP)		●		
Hungary	●	●	●	●
Lebanon				●
Luxembourg		●		
Mexico	❍	❍		❍
Poland	●			
Russia	●			
Slovenia		●		
Spain		●	●	
Ukraine	●	❍	❍	
United Arab Emirates	❍	❍	❍	❍

● Subordinate

❍ Peer/Partner

Source: OECD (2014a), "2014 OECD Survey of National Schools of Government".

In the third type of relationship, the school maintains a formalised relationship with government, though it is institutionally autonomous. In this model the relationship is framed by a legal agreement, a memorandum of understanding (MOU), or other similar arrangement. Among OECD Survey respondents only ANZSOG conforms to this model.

Forms of institutional relationships

In terms of forms of institutional relationships, as shown on Table 5.2, all of the respondents describe their relationship as subordinate to another institution of government (with the exception of Mexico, Canada, and the United Arab Emirates).

In most cases, the relationships that exist are of the subordinate nature, either to a CoG institution, as is the case of Russia's Presidential Academy of National Economy and Public Administration, or a ministry responsible for the public administration. This is the case of Canada's CSPS. In most cases, the nature of the relationship may reflect administrative or budgetary considerations that prescribe ministerial responsibility for the organisation or its functional leadership. For example, Spain's National Institute of Public Administration (*Instituto Nacional de Administración Pública*) (INAP) is an autonomous body within the national government of Spain, though it is administratively attached to the Department of Finance and Public Administration (INAP, n.d.).

Two schools reported a peer or partner relationship with a CoG institution. This is the case of the United Arab Emirates' Mohammed Bin Rashid School of Government. In general terms, partner or peer relationships exist with a ministry responsible for the public administration in 18% of instances (i.e. Mexico, Ukraine, and United Arab Emirates), whereas this was the case in 27% of cases with a ministry responsible for the civil service (i.e. Canada, Ukraine and United Arab Emirates).

The partner-peer relationship also exists with institutions that have very different mandates, missions, and institutional frameworks. Thus, for example, both the United Arab Emirates' MBRSG and ANZSOG are post-secondary education institutions. Although established through the sponsorship of national governments, both are institutionally separate from government, though they maintain extensive relationships with government. Hungary's NUPS, though also established as a post-secondary institution is, for its part, institutionally part of Hungary's government and the relations it maintains with government are consequently much closer. Finally, a third model of peer-partner relationship is highlighted by Canada's CSPS. CSPS was established as a departmental corporation in order to provide it with a degree of administrative autonomy, including the authority to retain its revenue. However, CSPS works closely with its portfolio department, the Treasury Board of Canada Secretariat, other CoG institutions, and federal departments to fulfil its training and development mandate for Canada's federal public service.

Institutional autonomy

In addition to the considerations described above, the nature of the institutional relationships with the government also influences the autonomy of the schools of government. schools of government that are within a centre of government or ministry portfolio may have less administrative and policy autonomy. This in turn may undermine their ability to directly define and adjust their learning programmes more quickly and easily, given the potentially lengthier approval processes. In other words, while access to centre of government institutions enables schools to be responsive to governmental priorities, it may at the same limit its ability to develop learning programmes in areas beyond these priorities. By contrast, where a school is established as an autonomous institution, it gains in independence and potential ability to achieve efficiency gains. Greater autonomy is usually accompanied by more decision making and resource management responsibility and accountability and, according to public management theories, is often associated with greater client satisfaction and responsiveness. It is also not found to lead to lesser collaboration with governmental and non-governmental stakeholders. Yet such gains may be negatively offset by less access to key governmental actors and potentially fewer links to government priorities. Whereas a model that is based on institutional autonomy may be ideal for schools of government modelled on higher education institutions, it may not be so for those that are the training organisations of government. In short, while there is no ideal model, it is important to consider the impacts of the model on the operations of the schools.

The finding of the OECD Survey suggests that there are varying degrees of autonomy among schools of government. Where schools of government have an academic mission, autonomy may be greater. However, where schools are institutions of government without an academic role, there appears to be a lesser degree of autonomy. This degree of autonomy may have an impact on the way in which schools interpret and act on the priorities of government in terms of their programming. This is particularly the case where centre of government institutions are the main point of contact. Therefore, as illustrated in Figure 5.3, the greater the degree of autonomy, the less influence CoG institutions will exert on the schools' priorities.

Figure 5.3. **National schools of government institutional autonomy**

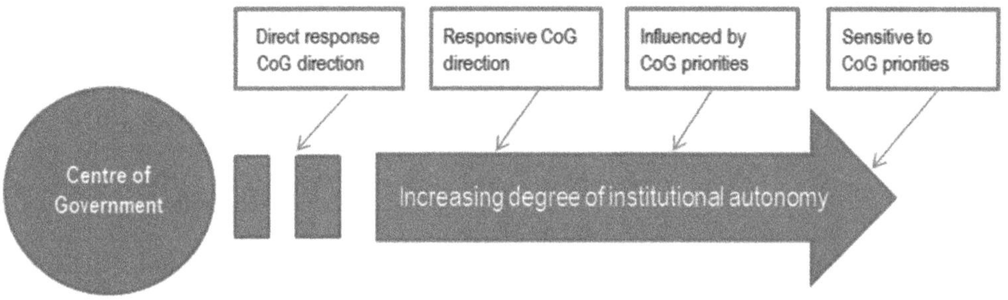

Source: Author's own work.

Importantly, several stakeholders associated the effectiveness of schools as learning institutions with the degree of closeness of the relationship to government and, in particular, a centre of government institution. Therefore, while autonomy of action is an important consideration, the ability to link schools with the broader priorities and activities of government requires a degree of proximity to the Centre (OECD, forthcoming).

Relationships with non-governmental institutions

In addition to their relationships with institutions of government, several of the responding institutions also maintain relationships with other educational institutions, primarily universities both at the national and international level. These arrangements vary considerably between schools, but include academic staff exchanges or joint appointments, collaborative design of programmes, or credentials recognition.

Examples of these collaborative initiatives include Mexico's National Institute of Public Administration (Instituto Nacional de Administración Pública), which has developed considerable relationships with universities across Latin America, in Europe and in Asia (OECD, 2014).[8] Spain's INAP is similarly engaged in activities in Colombia.[9] In Poland, joint learning programmes organised with post-secondary institutions have enabled the development and delivery of new curricula, such as programmes on migration jointly held with the University of Warsaw. Finally, another collaboration model is exemplified by ANZSOG, which as a consortium of government and academic institutions, is institutionally structured to leverage partnerships and collaboration as one of the institution's founding principles.

Legal framework

Another factor that influences the mandate and capacity of schools is their legal framework. For the most part, all of the responding institutions were established through a form of legal instrument, whether a law or decree. This is significant because the instrument gives legal life to the institution and is the source of authority for its mission and mandate. These legal instruments often provide the basis for regulations or policies that provide greater detail or specificity to the actions of the school. Furthermore, the powers that are granted schools in their constituent instrument may also have an impact on their capacity to engage with other institutions within government or outside. For example, the capacity for schools to sign partnership agreements with other institutions will be in most cases defined in the founding legislation. The clarity that can be provided through a legal instrument can therefore be an important factor in the ability of the institution to deliver on its mandate. Box 5.3 shows the powers of Canada's CSPS.

Box 5.3. Canada School of Public Service Act (excerpt)

Powers

5. In carrying out its objects, the school has the capacity of a natural person and may:

(a) acquire, manage, maintain, design and operate training, orientation and development programs for civil service managers and employees, particularly for those in the public service, and acquire personal and movable property;

(b) assist departments, boards and agencies of the Government of Canada through programs, studies and documentation developed at the school;

(c) co-operate with other persons and bodies engaged in management and personnel development;

(d) contribute funds for the pursuit of research or other activities related to the theory and practice of civil service management and public administration;

(e) provide services and facilities to any person or government, and charge fees therefor as provided by section 18;

(f) license, sell or otherwise make available any copyright, trade-mark or other similar property right held, controlled or administered by the school;

Box 5.3. **Canada School of Public Service Act (excerpt)** *(continued)*

(g) enter into contracts, memoranda of understanding or other arrangements in the name of Her Majesty in right of Canada or in the name of the school;

(h) acquire any money, securities or other personal or movable property by gift or bequest and expend, administer or dispose of the property subject to the terms, if any, on which the gift or bequest was made; and

(i) do all things necessary or incidental to the attainment of the objects of the school.

Source: Government of Canada (2015), "Canada School of Public Service Act", Department of Justice.

The legal instruments of the OECD Survey respondents are presented in Table 5.3.

Table 5.3. **National schools of government legal authority (government institutions only)**

School of government	Legal instrument[1]
Academy of Public Administration (Lebanon)	Article 49 of Budget Law 497 (2003)
Academy of Public Administration (Slovenia)	Civil Servants Act (2002)
Academy of Public Administration (Ukraine)	Presidential decree (1995)
Academy of Public Administration under the President of the Republic of Kazakhstan	Decree n°698 of the President of the Republic of Kazakhstan (2008)
CSPS (Canada)	Canada School of Public Service Act (2004)
EKDDA (Greece)	Law 1388 (1983)
ENAP (Brazil)	Presidential Decree n° 93.277 (1986)
ESAP (Colombia)	Law 19 (1958)
INAP (Mexico)	Constitutive Act and articles of association (1955)
KSAP (Poland)	National School of Public Administration Act (1991)
LSPA (Latvia)	Resolution of the Cabinet of Ministers (1993)
NUPS (Hungary)	National University of Public Service Act (2012)
SNA (Italy)	Decree of the President of the Italian Republic n°3 (1957)

1. The titles of the constituent or instruments were provided in English by the reporting institution.

Source: OECD (2014a), "2014 OECD Survey of National Schools of Government" and supplementary information provided by schools.

The legal instruments that define the existence and powers of the schools of government fall into two broad categories: laws of general application to the public administration as a whole and constituent laws specific to the institution and its establishment. The choice of legal instrument to establish a school of government is largely dependent on constitutional, legal, or administrative considerations proper to each country. However, having specific legislation to establish a national civil service learning and training institution may provide the necessary authority and mandate to engage with other government institutions and may serve as a precondition for the development of the necessary capacities. The reasons for this stem from the need for clarity about the institution's form, mandate, and mission, which may at times be overshadowed by other concerns in a law of general application.

Schools of government co-ordination mechanisms

One of the main elements highlighted by the OECD Survey is the degree to which schools of government maintain a multiplicity of relationships. These relationships may exist with national government institutions, sub-national levels of government, non-governmental institutions, other training and higher education institutions. In some cases these relationships extend to the international scene. This suggests the necessity to have in place co-ordination mechanisms to effectively manage these relationships.

Co-ordination at the sub-national level

Reflecting the organisation of their national civil services, the activities and responsibilities of schools may extend to supporting learning and development in civil services at the sub-national level, in addition to their mandate at the national government level. As shown in Figure 5.4, only Canada's Canada School of Public Service and Austria's Federal Academy of Public Administration (Verwaltungsakademie des Bundes) provide training solely at the national level. Most schools, such as France's National School of Administration (École nationale d'administration) (ENA), focus their activities at all levels of government. This is consistent with ENA's role as a civil service institution (École de service public) and its mission to train individuals for the non-technical[10] civil service in France and abroad (École nationale d'administration, 2016)[11] (see Box 5.4).

The main determining factor that may influence the activities of schools at other levels of government is the nature of the system of government. Where schools exist in unitary or centralised states these may have broader mandates at the sub-national level than schools in federal systems such as Australia and Canada. In the Australian case, though a federal state, as ANZSOG is a bi-national institution and its activities at the sub-national level are principally defined by its organisation as a consortium that includes state and territorial governments.

The role played by schools in offering training to audiences outside of government is also significant. In the cases of Hungary's NUPS or the United Arab Emirates' MBRSG, these activities are consistent with their status as post-secondary institutions. However, in the case of the United Kingdom's Civil Service College, its status as a private sector entity with a commercial mandate enables it to offer its services to a broad clientele (see Box 5.5).

Figure 5.4. **National schools of government training activities at the national and sub-national level**

Q. Are you providing training and learning at the national/sub--national level?

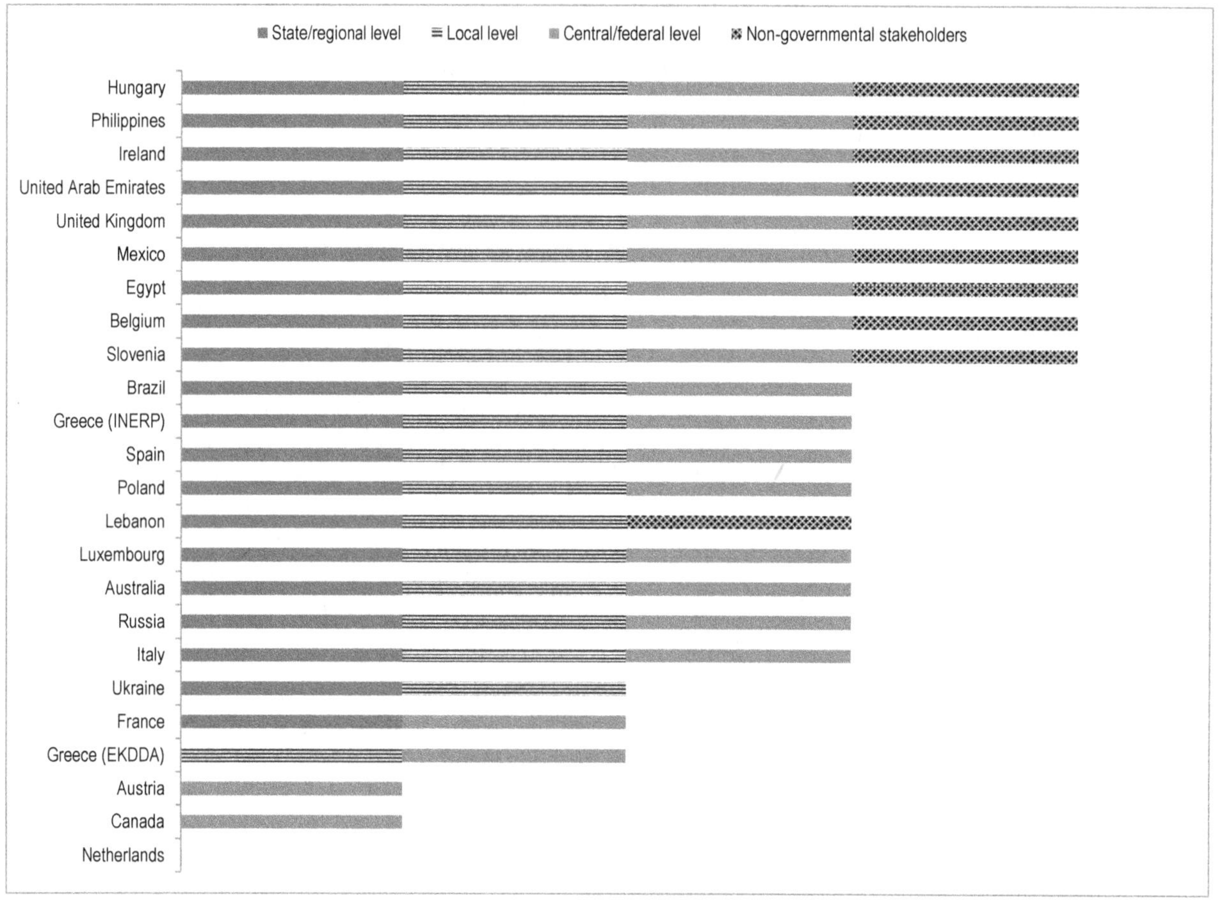

Source: OECD (2014a), "2014 OECD Survey of National Schools of Government".

Box 5.4. France's École nationale d'administration and its mission

The National School of Administration (*École Nationale administration* [ENA]) has as its mission to prepare for the highest levels of the non-technical civil service in France and abroad, and to prepare its students for their future responsibilities in France, Europe or elsewhere abroad.

The school offers diversified educational programmes, adapted to each stage of a professional career, be it the principal curriculum, continuing education or tailor-made programmes.

Source: École nationale d'administration (2016), "Les missions de l'ENA", www.ena.fr/eng/L-ENA-se-presente/Qui-sommes-nous/Missions-de-l-ENA.

Box 5.5. **United Kingdom's Civil Service College (excerpt)**

While our principal focus is on working with the civil service and wider civil service, our knowledge and experience of the workings of government is attractive to organisations across all sectors in the United Kingdom and to overseas governments and organisations.

We work primarily within the civil service and across the whole of the wider public service. Our clients range from large government departments to executive agencies and smaller arms' length bodies. Our experience across the wider civil service includes the NHS and local government.

We also work with the Third sector and can help commercial organisations that need a better understanding of the complexities of working with government.

Source: Civil Service College (2016), "About us", webpage, www.civilservicecollege.org.uk/about-us.aspx.

Modes of co-ordination

The multiplicity of relationships that schools are maintaining, either across their national government, with sub-national levels of government, or with non-governmental institutions, highlights the necessity of effective co-ordination mechanisms. As shown in Figure 5.5, in countries where a single training institution is active across multiple levels of government (national, sub-national, and local) there appears to be no single preferred means of co-ordination, though regular interactions between levels of governments is the most frequent means of co-ordination mechanism. The results of these discussions may find themselves formalised in other co-ordination mechanisms such as MOUs, the second most frequently used mode of co-ordination. At the same time, joint development of learning strategies and joint identification of learning needs are rarer.

At the national level of the national government, i.e. with the other institutions of government, nearly two-thirds of OECD Survey respondents noted the existence of specific co-ordination arrangements, such as regular meetings (75% or 17 out of 23 respondents to this question), MOUs (used by 15 respondents) and joint learning plans (used by 7 respondents).

These modes of co-ordination may also reflect the nature of the institutional relationships described above. As a result, institutions that possess a degree of autonomy from government may have greater capacity to independently define their training and educational services in order to serve a more diverse clientele.

Three cases illustrate this point. Both Hungary's NUPS and Columbia's Superior School for Public Administration (*Escuela Superior de Administración Pública*) (ESAP) have broad mandates that include providing training and professional development to public servants at all levels of government and providing undergraduate and post-graduate education to non-public servants (National University of Public Service, n.d.; Superior School of Public Administration, n.d.). Though both have institutional linkages to their national governments and consequently provide learning and training that meets the needs of their governments, they also have administrative autonomy over many of their activities.

Figure 5.5. **National schools of government co-ordination mechanisms across levels of government with respect to civil service learning**

Q. Please describe any co-ordination mechanisms between various levels of government with respect to learning/capability building of future or current civil servants

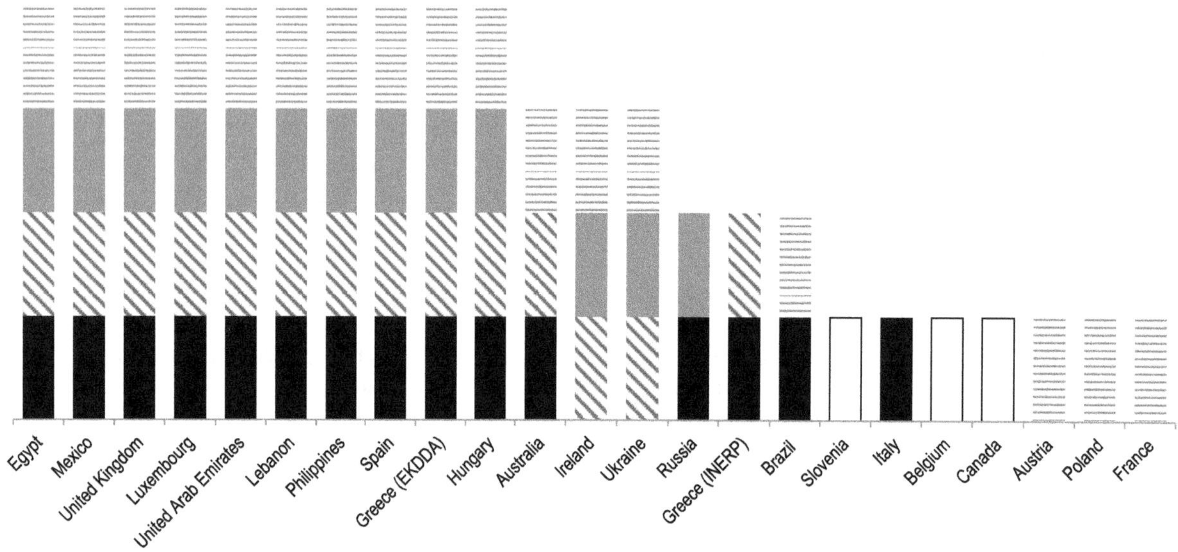

Source: OECD (2014a), "2014 OECD Survey of National Schools of Government".

By contrast, the Canada School of Public Service's mandate focuses mainly on enabling learning opportunities (e.g. courses and programmes) for federal public service employees. Therefore, unlike ESAP or NUPS, as an institution CSPS' main focus is serving the priorities of its portfolio ministry and those of government. Similarly, it can focus its activities on a single clientele within a single level of government. Thus, in the case of Hungary and Colombia, there is broader scope to provide learning services to other levels of government and other sectors, and hence the need for co-ordination, while in the case of Canada, this is more limited. Hence, the broader the autonomy of an institution and its mandate, the greater the need for co-ordination arrangements.

Schools of government internal governance and management

Internal governance and management are among the many factors that contribute to the organisational success of schools of government. Having in place the right structures, the right people, and clarity around the roles and responsibilities of each actor in management and governance are essential (OECD, 2015).

The OECD Survey findings highlight the existence of several internal governance and management models of participating schools, which models reflect a variety of factors such as the schools' legal structures, institutional model (i.e. academic versus public administration), relationships or partnerships with other institutions, and any requirements to engage with stakeholders across government or external to it.

As shown in Table 5.4, in almost 90% of cases (out 16 of 18 respondents to this question) the principal management structure of a school consists of leadership under an institutional head. By contrast, in a smaller number of cases, a board of directors/trustees and/or a council of members are the main governance or management body (4 and 5 out of 18 respondents, respectively). However, in several cases the management and governance structure is composed of several bodies, typically a head of institution and a board of directors/trustees. This approach serves to separate the division of duties between day-to-day administration under the head of institution, and strategy under the board of directors.

Table 5.4. **National schools of government internal governance and management structures**

Q. Please indicate who is responsible for the management of the school.

Country	Institution	Management body type	Institution type
Australia	ANZSOG	Head of institution	National school of government[1]
Austria	Verwaltungsakademie des Bundes(VAB)	Board of trustees/directors	National schools of government / Academy of public service
Belgium	Institut de formation de l'administration fédérale (IFA)	Head of institution and Council of members	National schools of government / Academy of public service
Brazil	Escola nacional de administração pública (ENAP)	Board of directors/trustees and Head of institution	National schools of government / Academy of public service
Canada	Canada School of Public Service (CSPS)	Head of institution	National schools of government / Academy of public service
France	École nationale d'administration (ENA)	Board of trustees/directors and Head of institution	University or other institution of post-secondary education
Greece	National Centre for Public Administration and Local Government (EKDDa)	Board of trustees/directors and Head of institution	National schools of government / Academy of public service
Hungary	Nemzeti Közszolgálati Egyetem (NUPS)	Council of members and Head of institution	National schools of government / Academy of public service and University or other institution of post-secondary education
Italy	Scuola Nazionale dell'Amministrazione		National schools of government / Academy of public service
Lebanon	École nationale d'administration	Head of institution	National schools of government / Academy of public service
Luxembourg	Institut national d'administration publique (INAP)	Head of institution and other	National schools of government / Academy of public service
Mexico	Instituto Nacional de Administración Pública (INAP)	Head of institution	National schools of government / Academy of public service
Poland	Krajowa Szkoła Administracji Publicznej (KSAP)	Council of members and Head of institution	National schools of government / Academy of public service
Russia	Russian Presidential Academy of National Economy and Public Administration (RANEPA)	Head of institution	National schools of government / Academy of public service
Slovenia	Upravna akademija (UA)	Head of institution	National schools of government / Academy of public service
Spain	Instituto Nacional de Administración Pública (INAP)	Head of institution	National schools of government / Academy of public service
Ukraine	National Academy for Public Administration under the President of Ukraine (NAPA)	Council of members and Head of institution	National schools of government / Academy of public service
United Arab Emirates	Mohammed Bin Rashid School of Government (MBRSG)	Board of trustees/directors and Head of institution	University or other institution of post-secondary education

1. ANZSOG is formally structured as a not-for-profit company owned by a consortium of governments and universities. It is regarded as a national school of government, distinct from schools at specific universities or training bodies within member governments.

Source: OECD (2014a), "2014 OECD Survey of National Schools of Government".

However, in only a few instances is the head of institution also a member of the board of directors, meaning that there exists no formal link between administration and strategy through the governance structure. Examples of this model include ANZSOG, Luxembourg's INAP and Poland's KSAP (see Box 5.6).

Box 5.6. **Governance of the Polish Academy of Public Administration (KSAP)**

Director

Appointed by the Prime Minister and responsible for the day-to-day administration of the Academy.

Council

It supports the implementation of KSAP's mission in the field of development and the lines of action for the school, additionally overseeing the compliance of the programme with the requirements of, and the challenges facing, public administration in Poland. The Council is empowered:

- to review and issue opinions on the directions of action followed by KSAP, the general rules of recruitment, the training process, as well as the functioning of the school and its effectiveness
- to recommend changes and present proposals in the areas referred to above
- to specify its own organisation and rules of procedure.

Source: Polish Academy of Public Administration's (KSAP) (n.d.), "KSAP", http://ksap.gov.pl/ksap/en/ksap/history-of-ksap (accessed 9 September 2016).

Another important factor in the management and governance of schools is the degree of their affiliation or relationship with other stakeholders. The presence of key governmental and non-governmental stakeholders on a board of directors or council of members may be an indication of close collaboration and interaction between the school and these bodies. Similarly, the presence of government officials on a board of directors would be conducive to greater collaboration between government and the school. For example, the Board of Trustees of the United Arab Emirates' MBRSG includes high-level representation of key ministries, non-departmental government entities, and the private sector (Mohammed Bin Rashid School of Government, n.d.). In the case of ANZSOG, its Board of Directors reflects the make-up of the institution as a consortium of government and academic institutions from both Australia and New Zealand. This ensures that the management of the school is attentive to the needs of all of its members (Australia New Zealand School of Government, n.d). At the same time, maintaining sufficient autonomy over the daily decisions concerning the operations of the school (e.g. staff policies, nature of the programmes) has also been cited as important to enhance efficiency, transparency, programme quality and responsiveness to client needs.

Assessment and recommendations

This chapter highlighted several factors that may impact the ability of schools of government to play a central role in developing civil service capacity to respond to different internal and external pressures. Foremost, there is a need to ensure that schools of government are provided with clarity of mandate. All of the schools of government that responded to the OECD Survey were established pursuant to a legal instrument. Looking ahead and concurrent with any planned legislative reviews and evaluations, countries may consider evaluating the legislation for clarity of schools' mandates, roles and responsibilities.

An important factor that affects schools of government operations and functions is the nature of their relationship with government institutions and in particular those at the centre of government. As institutions, schools of government exist to provide learning and training programmes with the aim of increasing the capacity of civil service staff to do their jobs in response to government priorities. The ability of schools of government to deliver on their mandates is therefore determined by their level of access to governmental priorities. As a result, even where the institutional linkages between schools and government are strong and well established, it may be at times necessary to clarify these so that these support the free and effective exchange of information. In addition, the attachment to the CoG may be indicative of a high governmental priority accorded to civil service training and development. At the same time, the relationships that schools maintain with other government institutions also allow for the alignment of their programme offerings with government learning needs across a wide spectrum of civil servants.

Overall, the findings of the OECD Survey suggest that establishing clear and robust co-ordination is essential to ensure that learning and development programmes are provided in a fashion that strengthens the capacity of the civil service, especially for institutions with higher degrees of autonomy.

Finally, the OECD Survey highlights the existence of different governance models among schools of government. Here again, this may be explained by differing national contexts and policy preferences about governance, management and administration. More important is the degree to which the governance model ensures the proper and efficient administration of the institution. Again, clarity about the governance model, especially where this can be described in the legal instrument establishing the school, is important.

In light of the above, schools of government may consider the following recommendations:

- **Recommendation 5.1**: Ensure clarity of schools' mandates, roles and responsibilities for providing civil service learning and development programmes.
- **Recommendation 5.2**: Strengthen formal means of co-ordination between schools and institutions of national government and, where relevant sub-national governments through the use of a range of co-ordination means and methods. These co-ordination efforts should facilitate the effective communication of priorities and needs as part of the development of a whole-of-government approach to civil service learning and development.

- **Recommendation 5.3**: Develop robust mechanisms to ensure the alignment of learning programmes with the priorities of government in order to address the skills needs associated with learning programme development.
- **Recommendation 5.4**: Consider internal governance arrangements to facilitate the input of both governmental and non-governmental stakeholders in order to ensure responsiveness to government priorities, identify emerging trends and expectations and enhance schools' efficiency and transparency.

Notes

1. Degrees are formally conferred by a member university of the ANZSOG, as it is accredited to confer degrees in its own name, though ANZSOG is responsible for programme design.
2. In addition to ANZSOG, training for civil servants in Australia is provided by the Australian Public Service Commission (see www.apsc.gov.au/learn-and-develop) and in New Zealand the State Services Commission has a specific mandate for leadership and talent development (see www.ssc.govt.nz/).
3. Hungary's NUPS is jointly affiliated with the Prime Minister's Office and the ministries of Justice, Defence and Interior.
4. The Mohammed Bin Rashid School of Government also maintains relationships with the United Arab Emirates' Human Resources Authority and the Dubai Human Resources Agency.
5. Responsibility for INAP is shared between the presidency and the Ministry of Public Administration.
6. Responsibility for Ukraine's NAPA is shared between the Office of the Prime Minister and the Ministry of Public Administration.
7. Luxembourg's INAP is also affiliated with the Ministry of the Interior.
8. These institutions include Fundación Getulio Vargas (Brazil), Instituto Nacional de Administración Pública (Spain), Instituto Nacional de Administración Pública (Guatemala), National Office of the Civil Service (Uruguay), Latin American Centre for the Administration of Development (CLAD), Instituto Zuliano de Estudios Económicos, Políticos y Sociales (Venezuela), and Chinese Academy of Governance.
9. Universidad Sergio Arboleda.
10. This distinguishes ENA from other institutions that provide education and training for certain specialised fields or professions such as engineering.
11. The Centre nationale de la fonction publique territoriale (CNFPT), formally part of the French government, has specific responsibilities for training civil servants in France's regional (*territoriale*) administration.

References

ANZSOG (Australia New Zealand School of Government) (n.d), "About ANZSOG", www.anzsog.edu.au/ and www.anzsog.edu.au/about-us/about-anzsog (accessed 6 August 2016).

Civil Service College (2016), "About us", webpage, www.civilservicecollege.org.uk/about-us.aspx.

Civil Service Training and Development (2011), "Learning and Development Framework for the Civil Service, 2011-2014", Civil Service Training and Development, Ireland, http://hr.per.gov.ie/wp-content/uploads/2011/04/Learning-and-Development-Framework.pdf.

ENA (École nationale d'administration) (2016), "Les missions de l'ENA", www.ena.fr/eng/L-ENA-se-presente/Qui-sommes-nous/Missions-de-l-ENA.

Government of Canada (2015), "Canada School of Public Service Act", Department of Justice.

INAP (Instituto Nacional de Administración Pública) (n.d.), "Who we are and what we do", www.inap.es/presentacion-ingles (accessed 6 August 2016).

Mohammed Bin Rashid School of Government (n.d.), "About us", www.mbrsg.ae/ABOUT-US/Introduction.aspx (accessed 6 August 2016).

National University of Public Service (n.d.), "Facts and figures", National University of Public Service, Hungary, http://en.uni-nke.hu/nups/facts-figures/organisational-information (accessed 6 August 2016).

OECD (forthcoming), "National Schools of Government Network Annual Meeting 2016: Summary report", OECD.

OECD (2015), *G20/OECD Principles of Corporate Governance,* OECD Publishing, Paris, http://dx.doi.org/10.1787/9789264236882-en.

OECD (2014a), "2014 OECD Survey of National Schools of Government".

OECD (2014b), *Skills beyond School: Synthesis Report*, OECD Publishing, Paris, http://dx.doi.org/10.1787/9789264214682-en.

OECD (2010), "Human Resources Management: Country Profiles", www.oecd.org/gov/pem/hrpractices.htm.

Polish Academy of Public Administration's (KSAP) (n.d.), "KSAP", http://ksap.gov.pl/ksap/en/ksap/history-of-ksap (accessed 9 September 2016).

ReSPA (Regional School of Public Administration) (2008), *Civil Service Training Systems in the Western Balkans Region*, ReSPA, Montenegro.

Superior School of Public Administration (n.d.), "Functions", ESAP, Colombia, www.esap.edu.co/portal/index.php/functions/ (accessed 6 August 2016).

Chapter 6

Future priorities and challenges for national schools of government

Schools of government are operating in a context of rapidly changing needs and expectations on the part of governments, citizens and civil servants themselves. The new and complex challenges faced by countries (e.g. climate change, migrant crisis, etc.) will necessitate a workforce with new and agile skill sets. This context has driven learning and development to the top of the human capital agenda in most countries and across sectors of the economy. This chapter looks to the issues of the future priorities and challenges that schools of government will be facing in the near term, such as the availability of adequate funding and human resources, the need for enhanced interaction with government institutions in order to ensure the continued relevance of curricula and the development of monitoring activities to demonstrate actual results and impact for the investments made by governments in learning and professional development.

Introduction

Schools of government are operating in a context of rapidly changing needs and expectations on the part of governments, citizens and civil servants themselves. The new and complex challenges faced by countries (e.g. climate change, migrant crisis, etc.) will necessitate a workforce with new and agile skill sets. This context has driven learning and development to the top of the human capital agenda in most regions of the globe and across sectors of the economy.

As the findings of the 2014 OECD Survey of National Schools of Government ("OECD Survey") highlight, for the most part schools of government are well-entrenched institutions, able to play a central role in the development of civil services and contribute to the effectiveness and efficiency of government. Schools of government are not insulated from the challenges that all governments are also facing, but they also face challenges and opportunities that arise from their roles as learning and training institutions. To this end, this chapter reviews some of the challenges and priorities identified by the respondents to the OECD Survey.

Current priorities and challenges faced by national schools of government

Recognising the importance of learning for an effective civil service and delivery on citizen expectations, over 80% of schools (19 respondents) selected developing future civil service leaders as their number one priority (see Figure 6.1). In about half of the cases, the responding schools also indicated an increasing focus on promoting excellence in government services and policies (47% or 15 respondents), and to a lesser extent, developing careers of professionals who are new to the civil service (20% of respondents) and aligning with international standards. The schools also identified the need to further align civil service learning activities with the priorities of government (45% of respondents), which may suggest an increased awareness to link their activities to government priorities, also in the context of resource restraint. Overall these three priority areas are coherent with the core role of schools as learning institutions.

At the same time, schools have also been the object of reforms that affect how they define their priorities and operations in the near term. Several OECD Survey respondents noted that recent governmental reforms had had an impact on their priorities. For example, in Spain austerity had made civil service innovation one of INAP's priority areas, while in Canada austerity was driving new attention to e-learning and career transitions.

These trends are also linked to the challenges identified by the schools. As shown in Table 6.1, the four main challenges identified by the schools include: reduced financing; limited human resources; limited co-ordination with other civil service training institutions; and limited mechanisms for monitoring the impact of training initiatives.

Figure 6.1. **National schools of government priorities**

Q. What are your school's priorities for the biennium?

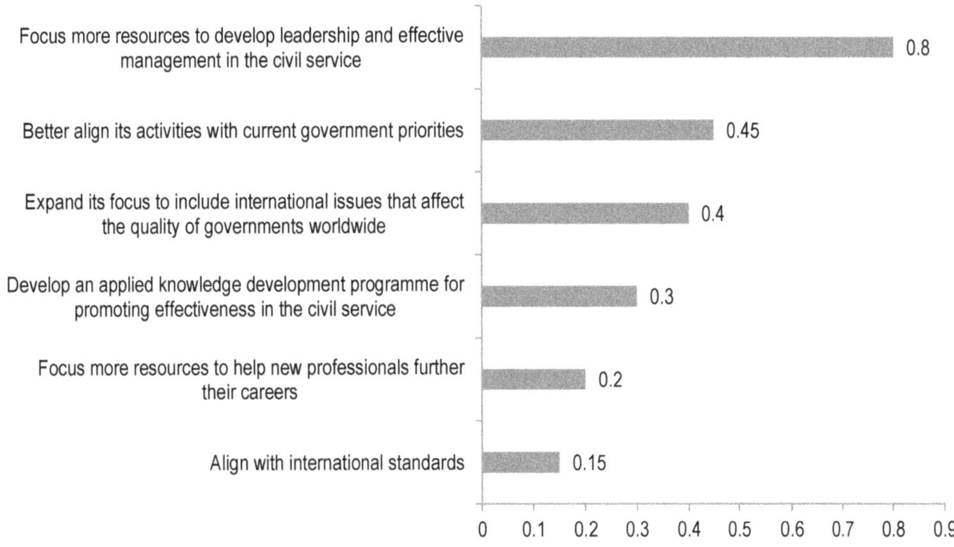

Source: OECD (2014), "2014 OECD Survey of National Schools of Government".

Table 6.1. **Challenges facing national schools of government**

Q. Please describe the main challenges facing the school

	Limited funding	Limited human resources	Limited capacity to identify government priorities	Limited capacity to identify learning needs	Limited capacity to identify skills necessary to deliver on government priorities	Absence of legal/policy requirement for civil service training/learning	Limited co-ordination mechanisms with other entities involved in civil service training and learning	Limited accountability mechanisms for civil service learning	Limited demand for research and knowledge development	Lack of mechanisms for monitoring the impact of learning/training initiatives	Lack of awareness of learning/ training opportunities
Australia	●	●									●
Austria							●	●			
Belgium	●	●	●	●					●		
Brazil	●	●	●	●			●			●	
Canada							●	●		●	●
Egypt	●					●	●	●			
France	●	●								●	
Greece[1]		●			●		●		●	●	
Hungary		●						●			
Ireland	●	●				●	●		●		
Italy	●	●		●		●					
Lebanon	●	●				●		●		●	●
Luxembourg	●								●		
Mexico						●	●		●		
Philippines[2]	●	●					●	●	●		
Poland	●		●	●	●			●		●	
Russia		●							●		●
Slovenia	●	●	●	●			●	●	●	●	●
Spain		●			●		●			●	
Ukraine	●										
United Kingdom	●									●	

1. Greece combines responses from both EKDDA and INERP.

2. Philippines also noted that the fragmentation in approach to training civil servants was a challenge.

Source: OECD (2014), "2014 OECD Survey of National Schools of Government".

Funding

Adequate resources are crucial for providing civil service staff with high-quality opportunities to learn and develop. At the same time, there is no single model within national schools of government for funding allocation. The outcomes of the use of those resources (financial, human and material) depend on the broader contextual factors, including efficiency; types of learning programmes; and of public servants trained, the quality of the resources and the way the resources are used.

Among OECD Survey respondents, 67% (15 out of 21 respondents to this question) reported limited funding as one of the main challenges facing the institution in the near future. These findings are broadly aligned with other surveys that show a downward trend in terms of funding for learning and development in the civil service. For example, figures reported by the Chartered Institute of Personnel and Development (CIPD) show that 51% of civil service organisations expected the funding for learning and development to decrease in the next 12 months (CIPD, 2015, p. 33). Indeed, 40% of OECD Survey respondents reported reductions in budgets and consequent reductions in staff. In parallel, the schools that reported no change in their funding over this period (53%) noted an increase in their functions.

An important factor in this regard is the funding model that applies to the schools, as this will have an impact on general income and, consequently, expenditures. Ultimately, financial considerations are central to issues such as the ability to staff the necessary complement of professionals to offer programmes. Given that 48% of the OECD Survey respondents reported contracting out for professional services to deliver their programmes, funding can rapidly become the prime determining factor of their activities.

Overall, the OECD Survey results show that there is recognition that investment in civil service learning can be instrumental in the ability of governments to respond to increasing citizen expectations. However, the ability to devote resources to staff development varies considerably across OECD member and partner countries and economies. Due to budgetary restrictions, capacity to fund the level of training required of civil services is also a challenge for some governments, particularly those that have instituted budgetary austerity. At the same time, while the impacts of the recent economic crisis on schools' budgets vary, it is evident that all schools of government need to be structured and managed efficiently to maximise limited resources.

As shown in Table 6.2, there is considerable variation in the funding available to schools of government to undertake their activities. While indicative of the general priority given to civil service learning, these findings should be interpreted with caution as they may be reflective of various factors, including programmes of study (e.g. degree diplomas vs. training), types of learning activities, efficiency of administration of learning, varying school mandates, different levels of staff and professional costs and different funding models.

Table 6.2. **National schools of government annual funding, 2014**

Country	Funding (in national currency)	Funding (in USD)	Number of civil service learners
APA (Kazakhstan)	KZT 1 548 272 000	USD 5 638 388	408
ANZSOG	AUD 16 000 000	USD 11 733 600	1 000
EKDDA (Greece)	EUR 22 000 000	USD 24 988 700	30 000
ENAP (Brazil)	BRL 20 000 000	USD 5 320 363	47 383
ESAP (Colombia)	COP 156 000 000 000	USD 54 542 280	11 800
INAP (Mexico)	MXN 41 000 000	USD 2 495 162	5 313
KSAP (Poland)	PLN 17 121 253	USD 4 608 207	3 880
KU Leuven Public Governance Institute (Belgium)	EUR 300 000	USD 340 755	848
IPN (Lebanon)	LBP 2 000 000 000	USD 10 876 161	3 000
LSPA (Latvia)	EUR 1 120 899	USD 1 806 299	5 233
National University of Public Service (Hungary)	HUF 16 384 943 000	USD 59 710 992	5 992
IPA (Slovenia)	EUR 400 000	USD 454 340	11 582
SNA (Italy)	EUR 18 116 000	USD 20 577 058	10 289

Source: Information provided by the listed schools.

In view of increasingly scarce resources, in the majority of cases, schools reported relying on a fee-for-service model to fund their training activities (see Table 6.3). In most cases, these fees are paid for by the employer – which is most often a governmental institution. Reductions in the learning budgets for governmental institutions may hence have an impact on the resource base of the schools. For example, in the case of Estonia, budgetary restraint led to abolishing the requirement for 2-4% of the annual payroll to be spent on training. Organisations thus freed from this requirement subsequently reduced their spending on training (Metsma, 2014). Moreover, across economic sectors, research in the United Kingdom suggests that larger organisations (defined as those with more than 250 staff) actually tend to spend less per employee on training than smaller ones, possibly explained by economies of scale. Therefore, if the civil service as a whole is anticipated to reduce its spending on training, this will likely have a direct impact on the funding for schools.

In very few instances are fees paid for by the learner or shared by the learner and employer. However, some of the training and learning activities do not entail a service fee, which could be interpreted to mean that the national school of government receives a form of base funding for its activities as part of the budget of the public administration, or benefits from an institutionalised levy on departmental or agency budgets to fund their activities.

In this regard some institutions have begun to consider alternatives to fee-for-service and cost-recovery models and are instead opting for a capitation model. Through this approach schools gain predictability in their budgeting and resource plans and can focus on developing and providing training specifically tailored for government, rather than compete with other providers on price for similar course offerings. For example, Canada's School of Public Service has recently begun phasing in such a funding model, starting in 2015-16 (Canada School of Public Service, 2015).

Table 6.3. **National schools of government fee-for-service income**

Q. Is there a fee for service?

	Training of future civil servants	Training of current civil servants	Training of middle managers	Training of senior managers	Leadership development
Belgium	❍	❍	❍	❍	❍
Brazil	❍	❍	❍	❍	❍
Canada[1]	●	●	●	●	●
Lebanon	❍	❍	❍	❍	❍
Luxembourg	❍	❍	❍	❍	❍
Mexico	♦	❖	♦	●	♦
Poland	❍	●	●	●	●
Russia	♦	♦	♦	●	❖
Slovenia	●	●	●	●	●
Spain	❍	❍	❍	❍	❖
Ukraine	❖	❖	❖	❖	●
United Kingdom	●	●	●	●	●

❍ No fee
● Yes, paid by employer
♦ Yes, paid by employee/student
❖ Shared

1. Canada has introduced a new funding model beginning with the 2015-16 fiscal year.

Source: OECD (2014), "2014 OECD Survey of National Schools of Government".

For schools this challenging operational environment is made more complex by competition from other private or training institutions. In this context, schools are likely to face double pressure – delivering more effective and responsive programmes in the context of reduced resources and budgetary pressures. While schools already committed to promoting innovation through teaching and research, greater investments are required to embed innovation into the ways schools operate and deliver their programmes (see Chapter 3).

Human resources

Another challenge identified by approximately 50% of OECD Survey respondents (12 out of 21 respondents to this question) concerns limitations in human resources. This factor also likely reflects a context of reduced financial resources. For example, a survey conducted in the United Kingdom by CIPD showed that 54% of civil service organisations anticipated reductions in staffing (headcount) in the areas of learning and development. Interestingly, 82% of respondents to the same survey anticipated increased workload, which may be seen as an attempt to "seek to 'do more with less'" (CIPD, 2015, p. 31).

As the OECD Survey reveals, the ability of schools to deliver on their mandates is to a significant degree dependent on having qualified staff as instructors as well as programme supports. Though OECD Survey responses varied with regard to the issue of staffing, most reported relying on a combination of full-time staff, consultants, and practitioners to offer their learning programmes. As noted above, these staffing pressures may require innovations in teaching techniques and, perhaps, a shift away from in-person instruction. At the same time, investments in human resources are important, as the quality of a school and its programmes cannot exceed the quality of its professors and instructors.

Indeed, the OECD Survey results reveal that reduced funding and human resources capacity appear to be at the core of many of the challenges that schools anticipate in the near future. In this context, schools may consider different models for service delivery including outsourcing to other organisations in the private or not-for-profit sector, or opt to focus on their core activities only, such as learning and development. Reduced funding and staff may provide an opportunity for schools to reinvent their approach to civil service learning. As discussed above, this may already be the case with the increased use of information technologies to support or provide learning programmes. For example, in the United Kingdom, e-learning is the key element of the UK government's training and development initiative, Civil Service Learning. Through Civil Service Learning the UK Civil Service has been able to provide high-calibre training to its staff, despite significant budget reductions.

Co-ordination mechanisms with other entities involved in civil service

As noted above, schools of government require sustained interaction with other government institutions in order to ensure the continued relevance of their programmes. Yet, 10 out of 21 respondents to this question noted limited mechanisms for co-ordination with other civil service bodies. This can significantly undermine the ability of schools to deliver on their mandates. As noted previously, ensuring effective co-ordination among the various government actors is essential to ensure the effectiveness of learning and training programmes.

Though the OECD Survey revealed a number of points of interaction between the schools and other government institutions, principally through meetings and other forms of direct interaction, these tended toward informal means of exchange and co-ordination. Faced with this challenge, schools may need to be increasingly proactive in seeking formalising the co-ordination of civil service training with other government institutions. This will be especially important as pressures on financial and human resources are likely to require increased efforts to streamline training and avoid programme duplications and overlaps. Ultimately, better co-ordination can also result in improving results and impact, and demonstrating increased value for money.

Mechanisms for monitoring the impact of learning initiatives

As noted in this report, one of the challenges faced by schools is demonstrating actual results and impact for the investments made by governments in learning and professional development. Given the pressures placed on all government institutions to demonstrate results, it will be increasingly important for schools to enhance their monitoring and impact evaluation activities. In the United Kingdom, notably, the Audit Office has already raised a concern about the results achieved by their civil service training (National Audit Office, 2011, p. 5). Given the increasing attention paid to demonstrating value for money, schools may also need to consider new means of evaluating their programmes. This means going beyond existing methods such as client satisfaction surveys and similar methods. As recommended previously, there is a need to broaden the scope of evaluation approaches, ensure that these evaluations consider impacts and outcomes, and include inputs from an array of interveners. Schools may also seek to work in collaboration with independent institutions and other government bodies, such as internal audit and evaluation units, to include wider sources of information into their evaluation of training programme impacts.

Assessment and recommendations

Since civil service learning policies and practices, invested resources, the learning environment, the mandate, governance and capacity of the schools and learning outcomes are interrelated, it is important to adopt a cohesive and systematic approach to the improvement of schools as public organisations in order to ensure their efficiency and relevance of their programme offerings to the needs of civil servants.

This chapter has shown that the years of economic crisis have had an impact on civil service learning and development activities, with a significant portion of schools having seen their budgets and/or staff numbers decrease between 2009 and 2014 (even though their structure has tended to remain unchanged and their functions have even tended to increase). In this context, and to continue to respond to government priorities, several schools aim to improve their programme offerings. This may involve re-orienting their activities towards areas with greater demand, skills gaps, less resource intensiveness, for example, by developing innovative approaches to learning and development. Schools also need to consider means by which they may become more cost-efficient. Further efforts will be increasingly important to adapt schools' curricula to changing civil service needs; to improve their capacity to engage and co-ordinate with other government institutions in the identification of priorities and in the development of whole-of-government training; and to demonstrate value for money through better evaluation of performance and impacts.

Looking to the future, the challenges and priorities identified through the OECD Survey suggest a number of possible avenues. Contending with this changing context also means that schools themselves will need to change in order to find ways to become more cost-efficient and provide greater value for money. Measuring accountability for these investments in training will also likely gain in importance, though this goes beyond just the responsibility of schools. Tackling these multiple considerations will require modernising their approach to learning and finding new ways of working.

Schools of government are subject to the same fiscal considerations as those faced by other government institutions. This means that they are subject to the same pressures to do more with less, like other government organisations. At the same time, the activities of schools and the learning budgets of government organisations are not explicitly linked. This may mean that during periods of fiscal restraint, budgets for training can be repurposed to other more pressing needs. Yet, without predictable funding the capacity of schools to deliver training may be undermined. Though the budget of schools cannot be completely isolated from the pressures that affect the fiscal framework, some countries are considering options that could enable greater funding predictability, such as the use of capitation formulas (e.g. Canada). This approach may also increase the accountability of the schools to ministries and departments by having to demonstrate how these funds have been used for training.

Financial predictability is also necessary to enable schools of government to make the transition to new learning methods. Though still heavily invested in traditional classroom teaching, schools are at the same time investing in new learning methodologies such as information and communications technology (ICT) enabled learning. In addition to its financial implications, this transition will also have impacts on the staffing needs of the schools. Until the transition to new learning technologies is completed, schools will also have to retain on staff the expertise that sustains existing programmes. Moreover, the transition to ICT will not lessen the need to retain subject matter and learning expertise.

In light of the above, schools of government and government should consider the following recommendations:

- **Recommendation 6.1**: Explore options to provide for greater predictability in the funding models of schools of government in order to fulfil their missions and mandates.
- **Recommendation 6.2**: Consider undertaking schools' capability reviews in order to align human, financial and material resources with the current and future requirements for learning and development, which would meet the needs of current and future civil servants and would support the development of necessary skills.

References

Canada School of Public Service (2015), *Report on Plans and Priorities 2015-2016,* Canada School of Public Service, Ottawa.

CIPD (Chartered Institute of Personnel and Development) (2015), *Learning and Development 2014: Annual Survey Report*, CIPD, London.

Metsma, M. (2014), "The impact of cutback management on civil-service training: The case of Estonia", *Administrative Culture* (151), pp. 58-79.

National Audit Office (2011), "Identifying and meeting Central Government's skills requirements", National Audit Office, London, United Kingdom.

OECD (2014), "2014 OECD Survey of National Schools of Government".

Further reading

ANZSOG (Australia New Zealand School of Government) (n.d), "About ANZSOG", www.anzsog.edu.au/ and www.anzsog.edu.au/about-us/about-anzsog (accessed 6 August 2016).

Australian Public Service Commission (2014), *State of the Service Report: State of the Services Series 2013-2014*, Australian Public Service Commission, Canberra.

Australian Public Service Commission and Australian National Audit Office (2003), "Building Capability: A Framework for Managing Learning and Development in the APS", Australian Public Service Commission.

Boud, D. and P. Hager (2011), "Re-thinking continuing professional development through changing metaphors and location in professional practice", *Studies in Continuing Education,* 34(1), pp. 17-30, http://dx.doi.org/10.1080/0158037X.2011.608656.

Cabinet Office (2014), *Civil Service People Survey 2014*, Cabinet Office, London, United Kingdom.

Canada School of Public Service (2015a), *Report on Plans and Priorities 2015-2016,* Canada School of Public Service, Ottawa.

Canada School of Public Service (2015b), "On-line courses", https://idp.csps-efpc.gc.ca/idp/login-en.jsp.

CIPD (Chartered Institute of Personnel and Development) (2015), *Learning and Development 2014: Annual Survey Report*, CIPD, London.

CIPD (Chartered Institute of Personnel and Development) (2016), "Factsheets: Induction programmes", www.cipd.co.uk/hr-resources/factsheets/induction.aspx.

Civil Service College (2016), "About us", webpage, www.civilservicecollege.org.uk/about-us.aspx.

Civil Service Human Resources (2015), "Civil Service Competency Framework 2012-2017", Civil Service Human Resources, London, United Kingdom.

Civil Service Training and Development (2011), "Learning and Development Framework for the Civil Service, 2011-2014", Civil Service Training and Development, Ireland, http://hr.per.gov.ie/wp-content/uploads/2011/04/Learning-and-Development-Framework.pdf.

Deloitte (2015), *Global Human Capital Trends 2015: Leading in the New World of Work*, Deloitte University Press.

Dickinson, H. (2013), "The 21st century public servant", *The Guardian*, 30 April, www.theguardian.com/society/2013/apr/30/21st-century-public-service-skills.

Dickinson, H. and H. Sullivan (2014), *Imagining the 21st Century Public Service Workforce,* University of Melbourne, Melbourne, http://bespoke-production.s3.amazonaws.com/msog/assets/b7/d2ec80db6d11e58244af312943873d/MSoG-21c-Draft2_2_.pdf.

Dobos, A. (2015), "Professional development in the civil service - From American and Hungarian perpectives", *Procedia - Social and Behaviourial Sciences*, 191, pp. 1886-18890, http://dx.doi.org/10.1016/j.sbspro.2015.04.706.

ENA (École nationale d'administration) (2016), "Les missions de l'ENA", www.ena.fr/eng/L-ENA-se-presente/Qui-sommes-nous/Missions-de-l-ENA.

Goldsmith, M. and L. Carter (2009), *Best Practices in Talent Management: How the World's Leading Corprations Develop and Retain Top Talent*, Wiley, London.

Government of British Columbia (n.d.), "Development the Best: A Corporate Learning Strategy for the BC Public Service", Public Service Agency, Victoria, British Columbia, www2.gov.bc.ca/local/myhr/documents/learning_education/corporate_learning_strategy.pdf.

Haruna, P. F. and S. Vyas-Doorgrapersad (2014), "Building public service capacity for development management: Reflections on a professional public administrationand training in African nations", *Journal of Public Affairs Education*, 20(4), 451-455.

HR Council (n.d), "HR Policies & Employment Legislation", http://hrcouncil.ca/hr-toolkit/professional-development.cfm (accessed 28 May 2015).

Im, T. and H. Shin (2000), "Evaluating training and development for Korean civil servants: Challenges and responses", *Progress, Problems, Prospects of Governance and Evidence-Based Government in Asia.* Seoul National Univesity.

INAP (Instituto Nacional de Administración Pública) (n.d.), "Who we are and what we do", www.inap.es/presentacion-ingles (accessed 6 August 2016).

International Labour Office (2010), *A Skilled Workforce for Strong, Sustainable and Balanced Growth: A G20 Training Strategy*, International Labour Office, Geneva.

Kirkpatrick, D. and J. Kirkpatrick (2009), *Evaluating Training Programs*, Berrett-Koehler Publishers.

Lee Kwan Yew School of Public Policy (2013), "About us", webpage.

Manning, N., J. Watkins and N. Degnarain (2012), "Public sector HRM system and staff performance", *GET Note*, December.

Medland, D. (2013), "Working in the public sector: Enterpreneurial skills top the wanted list", *The Financial Times*, 17 March, www.ft.com/cms/s/0/af6f5f9e-9186-11e2-b839-00144feabdc0.html#axzz3nhlqiPVv.

Menix, K.D. (2007), "Evaluation of learning and program effectiveness", *J Contin Educ Nurs,* 38(5), pp. 201-8.

Metsma, M. (2014), "The impact of cutback management on civil-service training: The case of Estonia", *Administrative Culture* (151), pp. 58-79.

Mohammed Bin Rashid School of Government (n.d.), "About us", webpage, www.mbrsg.ae/ABOUT-US/Introduction.aspx (accessed 6 August 2016).

Nason, E. and M. O'Neill (2015), "What metrics? On the utility of measuring the performance of policy research: An illustrative case and alternative from Employment and Social Development Canada", *Canadian Public Administration*, *58*(1), pp. 138-160.

National Audit Office (2011), "Identifying and meeting Central Government's skills requirements", National Audit Office, London, United Kingdom.

National Education Association (2013), "NEA Policy Statement on Digital Learning", National Education Association, www.nea.org/home/55434.htm.

National University of Public Service (n.d.), "Facts and figures", National University of Public Service, Hungary, http://en.uni-nke.hu/nups/facts-figures/organisational-information (accessed 6 August 2016).

Needham, C. and C. Mangan (2015), *The 21st Century Public Servant*, Public Sector Academy, University of Birmingham, Birmingham, http://pure-oai.bham.ac.uk/ws/files/27714134/The_21st_century_public_servant_working_at_three_boundaries_of_public_and_private.pdf.

OECD (forthcoming), "National Schools of Government Network Annual Meeting 2016: Summary report", OECD.

OECD (2015a), "Charting skills needs for a 21st century public sector", discussion note for the meeting of the OECD Working Party on Public Employment and Management on 20-21 April 2015.

OECD (2015b), *G20/OECD Principles of Corporate Governance,* OECD Publishing, Paris, http://dx.doi.org/10.1787/9789264236882-en.

OECD (2015c), "Policy shaping and policy making: The governance of inclusive growth", OECD Ministerial Meeting, www.oecd.org/governance/ministerial/the-governance-of-inclusive-growth.pdf.

OECD (2015d), *Government at a Glance 2015*, OECD Publishing, Paris, http://dx.doi.org/10.1787/gov_glance-2015-en.

OECD (2015e), *Building on Basics*, OECD Publishing, Paris, http://dx.doi.org/10.1787/9789264235052-en.

OECD (2015f), "National Schools of Government Network Annual Meeting 2015: Summary report", OECD.

OECD (2015g), "National Schools of Government Network", www.oecd.org/fr/gov/global-network-schools-of-government.htm (accessed 25 July 2016).

OECD (2014a), "2014 OECD Survey of National Schools of Government".

OECD (2014b), *Skills beyond School: Synthesis Report*, OECD Publishing, Paris, http://dx.doi.org/10.1787/9789264214682-en.

OECD (2011), *Public Servants as Partners for Growth: Toward a Stronger, Leaner and More Equitable Workforce*, OECD Publishing, Paris, www.oecd.org/gov/pem/publicservantsaspartnersforgrowth.htm.

OECD (2010), "Human resource management: Country profiles", www.oecd.org/gov/pem/hrpractices.htm.

OECD (2003), "Managing Senior Management: Senior Civil Service Reform in OECD Member Countries", OECD unclassified document, GOV/PUMA(2003)17, www.oecd.org/gov/pem/33708901.pdf.

OECD (1997), "Country Pofiles of Civil Service Training Systems", *SIGMA Papers*, No. 12, OECD Publishing, Paris, http://dx.doi.org/10.1787/5kml6g5hxlf6-en.

OECD (1997), "Public Service Training in OECD Countries", *SIGMA Papers*, No. 16, OECD Publishing, Paris, http://dx.doi.org/10.1787/5kml619ljzzn-en.

Office of Personnel Management (2015), "Federal Employee Viewpoint Survey Results: Employees Influencing Change - Governmentwide Management Report", Office of Personnel Management, Washington.

Phillips, P. (2010), *Measuring and Evaluating Training*, ATD Press, Alexandria, VA.

QAA (Quality Assurance Agency for Higher Education) (2016), "Higher Education Review", www.qaa.ac.uk/reviews-and-reports/how-we-review-higher-education/higher-education-review.

Quality and Qualifications Ireland (2015), "National Framework of Qualifications (NFQ)", www.qqi.ie/Pages/National-Framework-of-Qualifications-(NFQ).aspx.

Rajasekar, J. and S. A. Khan (2013), "Training and development function in Omani public sector organizations", *Journal of Applied Business and Economics*, 14(2), pp. 37-52.

Reichard, C. (1998), "Education and training for new public management", *International Public Management Journal,* 1(2), pp. 177-194.

ReSPA (Regional School of Public Administration) (2008), *Civil Service Training Systems in the Western Balkans Region*, ReSPA, Montenegro.

Smith, M. (2012), "How are the cuts affecting training", *The Guardian*, 23 January, www.theguardian.com/public-leaders-network/2012/jan/23/how-cuts-affecting-training.

Superior School of Public Administration (n.d.), "Functions", ESAP, Colombia, www.esap.edu.co/portal/index.php/functions/ (accessed 6 August 2016).

Treasury Board Secretariat (2014), "Highlights: 2014 Public Service Employee Survey", Treasury Board Secretariat, Ottawa, www.tbs-sct.gc.ca/psm-fpfm/modernizing-modernisation/pses-saff/hlr-rfs-eng.asp.

Treasury Board Secretariat (2008), "Policy on Learning, Training and Development", Treasury Board Secretariat, Government of Canada, www.tbs-sct.gc.ca/pol/doc-eng.aspx?id=12405.

UK Government (2014), "Building skills and competencies", Civil Service: Training and development (Guidance), 15 September, www.gov.uk/guidance/training-and-development-opportunities-in-the-the-civil-service.

United Nations Public Administration Network (n.d.), "Rethinking public administration: An overview", United Nations Public Administraton Network, New York, www.unpan.org/Portals/0/60yrhistory/documents/Publications/Rethinking%20public%20administration.pdf.

Victoria State Government (2015), "Using Digital Technologies to Support Learning and Teaching", *School Policy and Advisory Guide*, Victoria State Government: Education and Training, www.education.vic.gov.au/school/principals/spag/curriculum/pages/techsupport.aspx.

Wallace, S. (2009), *A Dictionary of Education,* OUP, Oxford.

Wilcox Johnson, D. (n.d.), "Evaluating training", *Thinking Outside the Borders*, pp. 17-23.

Wilson, K. and K. Boateng (2014), "Integrating ICTs into the teaching process: Issues in pedagogical practices in teacher education", *International Journal of Computing Academic Research*, 3(4), 96-103.

World Bank (2008), *Using Training to Build Capacity for Development - An Evaluation of the World Bank's Project-Based and WBI Training,* World Bank, Washington, DC.

Annex A

List of respondents to the 2014 OECD Survey of National Schools of Government

Country	Institution	Website
Australia	Australia and New Zealand School of Government (ANZSOG)	www.anzsog.edu.au
Austria	Federal Academy of Public Administration, Federal Chancellery of Austria	www.vab.gv.at
Belgium	KU Leuven Instituut voor de Overheid - Public Governance Institute	https://soc.kuleuven.be
Brazil	Brazilian National School of Public Administration	www.enap.gov.br
Canada	Canada School of Public Service (CSPS)	www.csps-efpc.gc.ca
Egypt	National Management Institute (NMI)	www.nmi.gov.eg
France	Ecole Nationale d'Administration (ENA)	www.ena.fr
Greece	Hellenic National Centre for Public Administration and Local Government	www.ekdd.gr
Greece	Institute for Regulatory Policy Research (INERP)	www.inerp.gr
Hungary	Nemzeti Közszolgálati Egyetem (NUPS)	http://en.uni-nke.hu
Italy	Scuola Nazionale dell'Amministrazione (SNA)	www.sna.gov.it
Ireland	Institute of Public Administration	www.ipa.ie
Lebanon	Institut des Finances Basil Fuleihan	www.institutdesfinances.gov.lb
Luxembourg	Institut national d'administration publique (INAP)	www.fonction-publique.public.lu/fr/structure-organisationnelle/inap/index.html
Mexico	Instituto Nacional de Administración Pública	www.inap.org.mx
Netherlands	Department of Public Administration, Radboud University Nijmegen	www.nsob.nl
Philippines	Development Academy of the Philippines	www.dap.edu.ph
Poland	Krajowa Szkoła Administracji Publicznej (KSAP)	www.ksap.gov.pl
Russia	Russian Presidential Academy of National Economy and Public Administration (RANEPA)	www.ranepa.ru/
Slovenia	Administration Academy, Ministry of Public Administration of the Republic of Slovenia,	www.mju.gov.si/si/upravna_akademija/
Spain	Instituto Nacional de Administración Pública (INAP)	www.inap.es
Ukraine	National Academy for Public Administration under the President of Ukraine (NAPA)	www.academy.gov.ua
United Arab Emirates	Mohammed Bin Rashid School of Government (MBRSG)	www.mbrsg.ae
United Kingdom	Civil Service College	www.civilservicecollege.org.uk

ORGANISATION FOR ECONOMIC CO-OPERATION AND DEVELOPMENT

The OECD is a unique forum where governments work together to address the economic, social and environmental challenges of globalisation. The OECD is also at the forefront of efforts to understand and to help governments respond to new developments and concerns, such as corporate governance, the information economy and the challenges of an ageing population. The Organisation provides a setting where governments can compare policy experiences, seek answers to common problems, identify good practice and work to co-ordinate domestic and international policies.

The OECD member countries are: Australia, Austria, Belgium, Canada, Chile, the Czech Republic, Denmark, Estonia, Finland, France, Germany, Greece, Hungary, Iceland, Ireland, Israel, Italy, Japan, Korea, Latvia, Luxembourg, Mexico, the Netherlands, New Zealand, Norway, Poland, Portugal, the Slovak Republic, Slovenia, Spain, Sweden, Switzerland, Turkey, the United Kingdom and the United States. The European Union takes part in the work of the OECD.

OECD Publishing disseminates widely the results of the Organisation's statistics gathering and research on economic, social and environmental issues, as well as the conventions, guidelines and standards agreed by its members.

OECD PUBLISHING, 2, rue André-Pascal, 75775 PARIS CEDEX 16
(42 2017 04 1 P) ISBN 978-92-64-26889-0 – 2017

www.ingramcontent.com/pod-product-compliance
Lightning Source LLC
LaVergne TN
LVHW081409110826
845149LV00010B/1680

* 9 7 8 9 2 6 4 2 6 8 8 9 0 *